# Check Your Christian Knowledge

# Check Your Christian Knowledge

TRIANGLE

First published 1993
Triangle
SPCK
Holy Trinity Church
Marylebone Road
London NW1 4DU



**British Library Cataloguing in Publication Data**

A catalogue record for this book is available from the British Library.

ISBN 0-281-04707-3

Typeset by Freestyle Graphics, Hereford
Printed and bound in Great Britain by
BPCC Paperbacks Ltd
Member of BPCC Ltd

# CONTENTS

# INTRODUCTION

The 1000 questions lying in wait on the following pages have been compiled from a wide range of different sources to test your knowledge on all sorts of Christian themes. Whether you are tackling one of the fifty specialist topics or pitting your wits against a set of broad-based general questions we hope you'll find something stimulating on every page.

From Dead Sea Scrolls to Liberation Theology and from medieval mystery plays to contemporary Christian broadcasting, the selection that follows provides hours of lively and thought-provoking entertainment. Art, music, saints, sinners, Bible studies, celebrated Christians from earliest times to the presentday, miracles, martyrs and movies - there are questions to satisfy anyone with an interest in Christianity past and present.

Some answers you may know right away, some you'll deduce, some you may not know at all and others may benefit from a little inspired guess-work. Whatever the quiz we hope there will be something to test, tax and just occasionally tease you as you check your Christian knowledge. Just in case you need them, all the answers are printed at the back!

You can use this book equally well on your own, or with family and friends. If there is a group of you, one can act as questioner, reading out one question at a time and awarding points to the first player to get the right answer. (With the multiple-choice 'Cross Section' quizzes you could try answering the questions without revealing the alternative answers, only resorting to these once all the players have exhausted their immediate powers of inspiration.)

Whatever your score and whatever your level of Christian knowledge, we hope you'll have fun working your way through this book.

# CROSS SECTION

1 **In which of these cities would you find frescos that constitute the oldest existing Christian art?**
a. Constantinople
b. Alexandria
c. Rome
d. Damascus

2 **By what name is 'the feast of unleavened bread' better known?**
a. Ascension
b. Whitsun
c. Passover
d. All Souls

3 **How many psalms are contained in the Book of Psalms?**
a. 170
b. 119
c. 111
d. 150

4 **Who was the author of *The Sandy Foundation Shaken* and *No Cross, No Crown*?**
a. William Penn
b. William Laud
c. William Wilberforce
d. William Williams

5 **To which city did Lot and his daughters flee from Sodom?**
a. Moab
b. Zoar
c. Gomorrah
d. Damascus

6 **Which of the twelve Apostles is symbolized by three moneybags?**
a. St John
b. Judas Iscariot
c. St Simon
d. St Matthew

7 **The Anglican Church in which country first officially suggested the holding of a Lambeth conference in 1865?**

a. Canada
b. Wales
c. New Zealand
d. England

8 **To which German university was Ferdinand Baur attached when the theological 'school' which bears its name was founded?**

a. Freiburg
b. Heidelberg
c. Dresden
d. Tübingen

9 **With which colour is the name Laban associated?**

a. Green
b. White
c. Black
d. Red

10 **Which is the seventh book of the Old Testament?**

a. Job
b. Judges
c. Joshua
d. Joel

# THE CHRISTIAN CALENDAR

1 Which day follows Shrove Tuesday?

2 How many Sundays are there in Advent?

3 When is the feast day of St George?

4 In olden days, Twelfth Night was a time of great celebrations on 5 January, preceding which Church festival on 6 January?

5 When is the feast day of the patron saint of children?

6 Pagan celebrations of the winter solstice were transformed and replaced by which important Christian festival?

7 How many Ember Days are there in the Christian year?

8 On which day in AD 1 can the Christian era be said to have begun?

9 What are the five Great Days of the Christian Year?

10 By what other 'botanical' name was Palm Sunday traditionally known in Britain?

# CROSS SECTION

1 **On which contemporary version of the Bible did J. R. R. Tolkien act as an editor?**
a. The New English Bible
b. The Jerusalem Bible
c. The Good News Bible
d. The Revised Standard Version

2 **When the fund known as Queen Anne's Bounty was formed in 1704, it restored to the clergy sums confiscated by which of her royal predecessors?**
a. James II
b. James I
c. Queen Mary
d. Henry VIII

3 **Who was the author of the pop prayerbook *Are You Running with Me, Jesus*?**
a. Bob Dylan
b. Malcolm Boyd
c. Diana Ross
d. Rex Reed

4 **In which country did the Maronite community originate?**
a. Egypt
b. Iraq
c. Syria
d. Malta

5 **What does the Hebrew name Malachi mean in English?**
a. Sage
b. My messenger
c. Teacher
d. My child

6 **Which Anglican cleric was the father of the real Alice in Wonderland?**
a. Charles Lutwidge Dodgson
b. Henry George Liddell
c. Lewis Carroll
d. Henry Parry Liddon

7 **Which was the most powerful of the twelve tribes of Israel?**

a. Simeon
b. Ephraim
c. Dan
d. Judah

8 **IHS is a monogram for whose name?**

a. Jesus
b. God
c. Mary
d. The Holy Spirit

9 **According to legend, which celebrated Quaker designed and made the first American flag?**

a. Benjamin Franklin
b. Paul Revere
c. Betsy Ross
d. Martha Washington

10 **Which religious sect was first led by Elder Jakob Amman?**

a. The Amish
b. The Evangelical Lutherans
b. The Arminians
c. The Assemblies of God

# THIS IS YOUR LIFE

1 For how many days was Albino Luciani pope?

2 This Baptist minister won a football scholarship to Illinois University, but he lost two US Democratic nominations to Walter Mondale and Michael Dukakis. Who is he?

3 Which Archbishop of Canterbury was beheaded on Tower Hill in 1645, having been found guilty of trying to 'overthrow the Protestant religion, and to act as an enemy to Parliament'?

4 What dramatic action did the CND campaigner Bruce Kent take in 1987?

5 Giovanni Bernadone was a young Italian gentleman whose love of the language and music of the troubadours gave him his nickname. What was it?

6 In which year was Billy Graham's radio programme *The Hour of Decision* first broadcast?

7 Which Member of the European Parliament staged a one-man protest in 1988 when the pope was due to address the Parliament?

8 Cardinal John Henry Newman was a leading member of which famous religious movement before he left the Church of England?

9 By what name was Pope John Paul II baptized?

10 George Carey's immediate predecessor as Archbishop of Canterbury was previously bishop of which diocese?

# CROSS SECTION

1 **What is the name of the route taken by Christ from Pilate's judgement hall to Calvary?**
a. Appian Way
b. Via Dolorosa
c. Stabat Mater
d. Via Cedrona

2 **Who was the teacher who stood trial in Dayton, Tennessee, in 1925 for teaching the theory of evolution, contrary to Tennessee law?**
a. William Bryan
b. John T. Scopes
c. Clarence Darrow
d. John R. Straton

3 **Why is a font so called?**
a. After the Latin for a spring of water
b. After the Greek for a basin
c. After the Old English for washing
d. After the Hebrew for healing

4 **How many theses on indulgences did Martin Luther nail to the church door at Wittenberg on 31 October 1517?**
a. 100
b. 12
c. 95
d. 60

5 **Albert Schweitzer is buried in the grounds of the hospital that bears his name, in which country?**
a. Guinea
b. Gabon
c. Guyana
d. Ghana

6 **This Polish priest died in Auschwitz on 14 August 1941, after offering to take the place of a friend selected at random to be put to death. On 17 October 1971 the man whose life he saved was among the congregation at his beatification. What was the priest's name?**
a. Francisek Gajowniczek
b. Maximilian Kolbe
c. Josef Korzeniowski
d. Teodor Konrad

7 **The Lord's Day Observance Society was founded in 1831 by the then bishop of which city?**
a. Calcutta
b. Chicago
c. Canterbury
d. Chester

8 **In which prison was John Bunyan incarcerated when he began writing *Pilgrim's Progress*?**
a. Durham
b. The Tower of London
c. Bedford
d. Norwich

9 **Which religious newspaper first appeared on 7 February 1863?**
a. *Church Times*
b. *The Tablet*
c. *Methodist Recorder*
d. *Christian Herald*

10 **Whose autobiography, *Surprised by Joy* (published in 1955), describes his conversion to Christianity?**
a. Gilbert Harding
b. Dwight Eisenhower
c. C. S. Lewis
d. Tennessee Williams

# MISSIONS OVERSEAS

1 Which disciple is mentioned as being the first to undertake a missionary journey?

2 Which sixteenth-century Catholic priest took missions to India, Japan and China?

3 During the course of his missionary work in Africa, who discovered the Victoria Falls?

4 Which seventh-century monk from Iona took an evangelistic mission to the North of England and became Bishop of Lindisfarne?

5 Which Spanish missionary sailed on Columbus' third voyage in 1498 and became known later as the 'Apostle of the Indians', having championed the cause of South American Indians against the Spanish authorities?

6. Who founded the Inn of the Sixth Happiness in Yangcheng, China in the 1930s?

7 By 1925 it was estimated that there were 21,000 Protestant missionaries operating world-wide. Approximately what percentage were North Americans?

8 In the 1730s John Wesley, the founder of Methodism, went on a disastrous missionary journey to which American state?

9 What was the name of St Paul's Jewish-Cypriot companion on his early missionary journeys?

10 Which twentieth-century medical missionary in Africa had previously published an authoritative study entitled *J. S. Bach, le musicien-poète*?

# CROSS SECTION

1 **Which Anglican priest became Gandhi's closest friend from the Western Christian Church?**

a. David Knox
b. Harry Edwards
c. Charles Andrews
d. Terence Latimer

2 **Who, in addition to Jesus, was born in Bethlehem?**

a. King David
b. St Luke
c. St John
d. Isaiah

3 **How long did Jonah spend in the belly of the fish?**

a. Seven days and seven nights
b. Four days
c. Three days and three nights
d. Ten days

4 **Who played the priest in David Lean's film *Ryan's Daughter*?**

a. Richard Attenborough
b. Donald Sutherland
c. Robert Mitchum
d. Trevord Howard

5 **Who is the patron saint of prisoners?**

a. St Leonard
b. St Peter
c. St Cyril
d. St Cyprian

6 **Which animal is used as an emblem of Christ's incarnation?**

a. The lamb
b. The unicorn
c. The lion
d. The deer

7 **Which of these charities was founded in 1953 by the City of London clergyman Chad Varah?**

a. Crisis
b. Shelter
c. Samaritans
d. War on Want

8 **Which of these is not one of the four cardinal virtues?**

a. Prudence
b. Temperance
c. Fortitude
d. Diligence

9 **Who was Moses' father-in-law?**

a. Joseph
b. Jethro
c. Joshua
d. Jeremiah

10 **In which Italian city did Leonardo da Vinci paint his celebrated *Last Supper* in 1498?**

a. Florence
b. Naples
c. Milan
d. Rome

# SAINTS ALIVE

1 Which eleventh-century saint was the founder of London's Westminster Abbey?

2 The Apostle St Andrew is the patron saint of Scotland and which other countries?

3 What is the principal flower associated with the Virgin Mary?

4 Which saint is invoked by those wishing to recover lost property?

5 Who was the first Archbishop of Canterbury?

6 Who wrote *Confessions* and *The City of God*?

7 Where is it thought that St George, the patron saint of England, was martyred?

8 Which fourth-century saint was not only the Emperor Constantine's mother but also instigated the excavations at Calvary in her search for the 'true cross'?

9 Which saint was reputed to be able to change poisonous snakes into stones?

10 St Kentigern was a friend of St Columba and often referred to as 'Mungo'. What does it mean?

# CROSS SECTION

1 **Where was Abraham born?**
   a. Jericho
   b. Ur
   c. Babylon
   d. Sidon

2 **Where was the land of Nod?**
   a. East of Eden
   b. West of Eden
   c. North of Eden
   d. South of Eden

3 **By what other name is the Song of Simeon also known?**
   a. Beatitudes
   b. Nunc Dimittis
   c. Magnificat
   d. Benedictus

4 **Monte Cassino, almost totally destroyed in 1944, was built as the principal monastery of which religious order?**
   a. Dominican
   b. Franciscan
   c. Benedictine
   d. Carthusian

5 **Where in the ancient world was St Nicholas once bishop?**
   a. Antioch
   b. Alexandria
   c. Myra
   d. Smyrna

6 **Who was the founder of Sunday Schools?**
   a. Lord Shaftesbury
   b. Robert Raikes
   c. William Temple
   d. William Wilberforce

7 **Who, according to Genesis, was a 'mighty hunter before the Lord'?**
   a. Enoch
   b. Uriah
   c. Nimrod
   d. Abimelech

8 **In which country did Gregory Lopez become the first native bishop?**
   a. China
   b. Brazil
   c. Mexico
   d. Philippines

9 **At which battle did the 'Christian League' defeat the Turks on 7 October 1571?**
   a. Tours
   b. Marignano
   c. Lepanto
   d. Constantinople

10 **Wagner's *Parsifal* tells the story of which celebrated sacred object?**
   a. Christ's Shroud
   b. The True Cross
   c. Christ's Crown of Thorns
   d. The Holy Grail

# CHRISTIANITY IN ART

1 Which artist painted limp watches, dream-like landscapes, collaborated with film-maker Luis Bunuel and who then, in 1951, painted *Christ of St John of the Cross*?

2 Who was commissioned by Pope Julius II to design his tomb, of which the statue of Moses is one of the most famous pieces?

3 Although trained as a painter, what medium did Graham Sutherland choose for his *Christ in Majesty* in Coventry Cathedral?

4 Which English mystical poet was also a highly gifted painter and engraver of religious subjects including *Illustrations for the Book of Job*?

5 What is the name given to the gold and silver covering applied to icons, leaving only the face and hands of the subject visible?

6 Which twentieth-century British sculptor was commissioned to create the well-known *Madonna and Child* in St Matthew's Church, Northampton?

7 Whose *Madonna and Child* was made for the church of St Ives, Cornwall, in memory of a son killed while serving in the RAF?

8 In what area of Asia Minor can we still visit several hundred cave-churches decorated with Byzantine rock paintings?

9 What is unusual about the way the Mother of God is depicted in the French town of Rocamadour?

10 Who painted *The Light of the World*?

# CROSS SECTION

1 **How many stones did David choose from the brook before he faced Goliath?**
   a. 12
   b. 6
   c. 5
   d. 10

2 **Which of these is the odd one out in the Bible?**
   a. Ephesus
   b. Corinth
   c. Thessalonica
   d. Athens

3 **Which Scottish-born American theologian published a translation of the Bible as well as becoming a professor at Union Theological Seminary, New York?**
   a. James Moffatt
   b. Dale Carnegie
   c. James McGready
   d. John MacArthur

4 **Who led an anti-religious campaign in the former Soviet Union in the period 1958-64?**
   a. Brezhnev
   b. Stalin
   c. Khruschev
   d. Kosygin

5 **From what material was Noah's ark constructed?**
   a. Cedar
   b. Oak
   c. Sycamore
   d. Gopher

6 **To what does the number 666 refer in Revelation 13.18?**
   a. The number of the beast
   b. The kings of the earth
   c. The saints rejoicing
   d. The number that were sealed

7 **To which denomination did Gerald Priestland, the BBC's religious affairs correspondent before 1982 and presenter of *Priestland's Progress* belong?**

a. Anglicanism
b. Methodism
c. Roman Catholicism
d. The Society of Friends

8 **Who is the patron saint of television?**

a. St Lucy
b. St Clare
c. St Apollonia
d. St Martha

9 **Who wrote the hymn 'Love divine all loves excelling'?**

a. William Dix
b. John Keble
c. Isaac Watts
d. Charles Wesley

10 **On which day were the earliest observances of Christmas held?**

a. 25 December
b. 6 January
c. 21 March
d. 21 September

# OLD TESTAMENT PROPHETS

1 When Isaiah had a vision of God in all his glory in the Temple, one of the seraphim flew to him and touched his mouth with something. What was it?

2 Why did Hosea's wife, Gomer, cause him so much anguish?

3 Having cast Daniel's companions, Shadrach, Meshach and Abednego into the fiery furnace, Nebuchadnezzar could see men walking unharmed through the flames. How many could he see?

4 Which prophet living in the eighth to seventh centuries BC spoke these words?

> *But you, O Bethlehem Ephrathah, who are little among the clans of Judah, from you shall come forth for me one who is to be ruler in Israel.*

5 Proverbially, a leopard can never change its spots. In the book of which Old Testiment prophet do we find this saying?

6 Ezekiel is taken by the hand to a valley full of dry bones and is commanded to prophesy. What is the result?

7 What had God commanded Jonah to do, which caused him to flee instead to Tarshish, during which voyage he ended up in the belly of a great fish?

8 In Isaiah 15 there is a pronouncement concerning Moab. From whom were the Moabites descended?

9 According to Hosea, those that sow the wind shall reap what?

10 In Joel 3.10 there is a verse exhorting people to 'Beat your ploughshares into swords and your pruning hooks into spears'. Whose famous words are being reversed here?

# CROSS SECTION

1 **How many relatives whom a woman may not marry are listed in the Table of Kindred and Affinity?**
   a. 12
   b. 25
   c. 18
   d. 9

2 **Which feast commemorates the institution and gift of the Holy Eucharist?**
   a. Corpus Christi
   b. Epiphany
   c. Advent
   d. Circumcision

3 **The *Ascent of Mount Carmel* was the earliest of his spiritual treatises. What was his name?**
   a. Peter Abelard
   b. Roger Bacon
   c. St John of the Cross
   d. Thomas Arundel

4 **In which year was the Service of Nine Lessons and Carols first broadcast by the BBC at Christmastide?**
   a. 1928
   b. 1918
   c. 1938
   d. 1948

5 **Traditionally how many corporal works of mercy are there?**
   a. 7
   b. 10
   c. 5
   d. 16

6 **Who was emperor of Rome at the time of Christ's birth?**
   a. Tiberius
   b. Augustus
   c. Nero
   d. Caligula

7 **In which year was the General Synod of the Church of England constituted?**
a. 1960
b. 1970
c. 1945
d. 1950

8 **On which mountain top did Abraham prepare to sacrifice Isaac?**
a. Nebo
b. Ebal
c. Hermon
d. Moriah

9 **Which is the ninth commandment?**
a. Thou shalt do no murder
b. Thou shalt keep holy the Sabbath day
c. Thou shalt not bear false witness
d. Thou shalt not covet

10 **In which city is the world's largest cathedral?**
a. New York
b. Florence
c. Rome
d. Salt Lake City

# WORDS OF WISDOM

1 Which theologian, suspected by the Gestapo of being involved in a plot to kill Hitler, had his written work from concentration camps posthumously published as *Letters and Papers from Prison*?

2 Which medieval theologian was referred to by his fellow students as the 'Dumb Ox', but by others as the 'Angelic Doctor'?

3 Which nineteenth-century philosopher, in reacting against rationalism, speaks of our having to make a 'leap of faith'?

4 'Give me chastity and continency - but not yet' are the words of one of the great early theologians and fathers of the Church. Who was he?

5 Which of today's chief black theologians in the USA includes among his work *A Black Theology of Liberation* and *God of the Oppressed*?

6. Which medieval mystic wrote *The Cloud of Unknowing*?

7 Who wrote these three essays: *The Appeal to the German Nobility, The Babylonian Captivity* and *The Freedom of the Christian*?

8 A medieval mystic wrote, 'all shall be well and all shall be well and all manner of things shall be well'. Who was she?

9 Who claimed that God transcends human attempts at description as he is the 'being beyond being'?

10 The doctrine of predestination was preached by which sixteenth-century French-born theologian?

# CROSS SECTION

1 **In which language did Brahms write his requiem?**
a. Latin
b. Italian
c. German
d. French

2 **On the road from Jerusalem to where did the good Samaritan find the wounded traveller to whose aid he came?**
a. Jericho
b. Hebron
c. Bethany
d. Lydda

3 **Where did the vision of the Virgin Mary first appear to Lucia dos Santos and others in 1917?**
a. Guadalupe
b. Pontmain
c. Seville
d. Fátima

4 **Who was canonized in 1946 to become the first American saint?**
a. Frances Brideau
b. Frances Bizzocca
c. Frances Lanel
d. Frances Xavier Cabrini

5 **In 1716 500 copies of a translation of the New Testament from Coptic into Latin by David Wilkins were published by Oxford University Press. How long did it take until the last copy was sold?**
a. 91 years
b. 191 years
c. 3 years
d. 61 years

6 **What was the title of Frederick William Rolfe's 1904 publication about a priest unexpectedly chosen for the papacy?**

a. *The Quest for Corvo*
b. *Hadrian VII*
c. *The Desire and Pursuit of the Whole*
d. *They Also Serve*

7 **What name did William Booth first give to the revivalist movement he founded in Whitechapel?**

a. Salvation Army
b. Christian Mission
c. Church Army
d. London Mission

8 **In which year was the United Reformed Church formed?**

a. 1972
b. 1962
c. 1952
d. 1922

9 **Which of these is the odd one out?**

a. Elizabeth Fry
b. Joseph Rowntree
c. George Cadbury
d. Samuel Mars

10 **Which pair of saints are known as the Apostles of the Slavs?**

a. Cyril and Methodius
b. Cornelius and Macarius
c. Constantius and Modestus
d. Cyprian and Maximus

# MIRACLES AND VISIONS

1 As the people of Israel followed Moses out of Egypt they were caught between their pursuers and the Red Sea. What miracle saved them?

2 St Francis and some other saints are said to have miraculously developed wounds similar to the Five Wounds of Christ. What are these marks called?

3 When Jesus sees Jairus' daughter he says she is not dead but she is - what?

4 What is the Beatific Vision?

5 At Pentecost, the Apostles were filled with the Holy Spirit and developed a miraculous ability. What was it?

6 Bernadette of Lourdes saw eighteen visions of the Virgin Mary in 1858. What original miracle occurred during this time?

7 After Jesus had fed the five thousand with five loaves and two fishes, how many baskets of left-overs were collected?

8 In Revelation John's apocalyptic vision contains four horsemen. What colour horses do they ride?

9 Two miraculous events are reported concerning the torture and death of St Catherine of Alexandria. What are they?

10 Who brought the Virgin Mary the news of the miracle of her conceiving and bearing 'the Son of the Most High'?

# CROSS SECTION

1 **Which was the first part of the Bible ever to appear in print, when it was published in Italy in 1477?**
a. Psalms
b. Genesis
c. Matthew
d. Acts

2 **Luke 16.22 refers to a place of special status for the good in the world of the dead. Where is it?**
a. Abraham's Bosom
b. Ephraim
c. Limbo
d. Hades

3 **Who is the patron saint of France?**
a. St Joan of Arc
b. St Martin of Tours
c. St Lazare
d. St Etienne

4 **Which video film, popular in evangelistic events, stars Pat Boone and tells the story of David Wilkerson's ministry among the street gangs of New York?**
a. *West Side Story*
b. *The Cross and the Switchblade*
c. *East Meets West*
d. *Where Angels Fear To Tread*

5 **Which famous Roman Catholic 'grouping' was first instituted in 1557 and survived until 1966?**
a. Latin sacraments
b. Index of Prohibited Books
c. Knights Templar
d. Palatine Guard at the Vatican

6 **Who was the ruling elder of the 101 passengers who sailed to America on the *Mayflower* in September 1620?**
a. John Smith
b. Abraham Flower
c. Nathaniel Walker
d. William Brewster

7 **Who was Laban's 'weak eyed' daughter who bore Jacob six sons and a daughter?**
a. Leah
b. Rachel
c. Martha
d. Elizabeth

8 **If Beersheba was the most southerly town in Palestine, which was the most northerly?**
a. Philadelphia
b. Dan
c. Hebron
d. Askelon

9 **Who did the Lollards follow?**
a. John Wycliffe
b. Thomas More
c. Hugh Latimer
d. Peter Lollard

10 **Which feast day was established by Odilo of Cluny to celebrate all who died in the Christian faith without suffering martyrdom?**
a. Corpus Christi
b. Trinity Sunday
c. Rogation Sunday
d. All Souls' Day

# WHO SAID?

1 Who quotes this simile in his ecclesiastical history to describe the brevity of a human life: 'One of the sparrows from outside flew very quickly through the hall; as if it came in one door and soon went out through another'?

2 Which fifteenth-century writer wrote 'Man proposes but God disposes'?

3 In which Epistle did Paul write, 'If I speak in the tongues of men and of angels, but have not love, I am a noisy gong or a clanging cymbal'?

4 Who said,'Here I stand, I can do no other. God help me. Amen'?

5 Whose words are these:'Just are the ways of God, And justifiable to men'?

6 What do these words mean, 'Eli, Eli, lama sabachtlani'?

7 Whose views on forgiveness are these: 'You ought certainly to forgive them as Christians, but never admit them in your sight, or allow their names to be mentioned in your hearing'?

8 Who cried out,'That unworthy hand! That unworthy hand!', thrusting his right hand into the fire as he stood at the stake?

9 Whose prayer is this?

*Lord, I am taking a stand for what I believe is right. The people are looking to me for leadership, and if I stand before them without strength and courage, they will falter. I am at the end of my powers. I have nothing left. I've come to the point where I can't face it alone.*

10 Which Apostle said, Silver and gold have I none; but such as I have I give thee'?

# CROSS SECTION

1 **Which Apostle was chosen, by the casting of lots, to fill the place vacated by Judas Iscariot?**
   a. Paul
   b. Matthias
   c. Stephen
   d. Timothy

2 **What is the title of the magazine supervised by Billy Graham which is one of the world's most widely-circulated religious periodicals?**
   a. *Decision*
   b. *Faith in the Future*
   c. *The Word*
   d. *The Message*

3 **How many locks were shawn from Samson's head on Delilah's instructions?**
   a. 2
   b. 100
   c. 50
   d. 7

4 **Which composer is often called the Father of Anglican Church Music?**
   a. Orlando Gibbons
   b. Henry Purcell
   c. Georg Friedrich Handel
   d. Edward Elgar

5 **In which year did the Convocation of Canterbury undertake a revision of the Authorized Version of the Holy Scriptures?**
   a. 1834
   b. 1929
   c. 1911
   d. 1870

6 **Which religious movement was founded by L. Ron Hubbard in 1954?**
   a. Christology
   b. Scientology
   c. Primitive Methodist Church
   d. Church of the Lord

7 **His mother was Maacah, his sister was Tamar and his father was David. Who was he?**
a. Absalom
b. Joshua
c. Saul
d. Uriah

8 **Who gained freedom from worship and full civil rights as a result of the Edict of Nantes?**
a. Jews
b. Cathars
c. Huguenots
d. Followers of all religions

9 **Which is the oldest complete copy of the New Testament?**
a. Codex Sinaiticus
b. Dead Sea Scrolls
c. Book of Kells
d. Vulgate Bible

10 **How was Elijah carried up to heaven?**
a. On a whirlwind
b. In a chariot of fire
c. By angels
d. In a ball of fire

# THE CHRISTIAN HERITAGE: CHURCHES

1 What name is given to the English Gothic style of ecclesiastical architecture dating from the late fourteenth century to the mid-sixteenth century displaying, for instance, vertical tracery in the windows?

2 What is 'clipping' the Church?

3 Where would you find what is reputed to be the oldest wooden-walled church in the world?

4 What was the 'rood screen' often found in medieval churches?

5 Who founded the chuch of St Mary the Virgin, Battle, East Sussex?

6 Before church clocks, how would people know when to attend services?

7 From which century did pews for the general congregation appear in churches?

8 What was the depiction of the Last Judgement, often painted over the chancel arch, called?

9 Cirencester and other fine Cotswold churches were the beneficiaries of wealthy cloth merchants and because of this they have a popular name. What is it?

10 In St Mary's Church, Selborne, Hampshire a stained glass window depicting St Francis preaching to the birds was installed in 1920. What does it commemorate?

# CROSS SECTION

1 **What is the term given in art to the image of Mary mourning the dead body of Jesus supported on her lap?**
   a. Lacrimosa
   b. Testimonia
   c. Pietà
   d. Ave Maria

2 **Why is a papal bull so called?**
   a. After the Latin for a command
   b. After the Latin for a seal
   c. After the Greek for a prayer
   d. After the Greek for a written document

3 **Where in the church are liturgical objects stored?**
   a. In the basilica
   b. In the clerestory
   c. In the sacristry
   d. In the baptistry

4 **Where was the Church of Jesus Christ of Latter-Day Saints founded in 1830?**
   a. Manchester, New York
   b. Manchester, New Hampshire
   c. Salt Lake City, Utah
   d. Manchester, England

5 **Which was the first of the ten plagues of Egypt described in Exodus?**
   a. River Nile turning to blood
   b. Death of the 'firstborn'
   c. Hail
   d. Gnats

6 **How many stations of the cross are there?**
   a. 12
   b. 14
   c. 16
   d. 20

7 **What was the trade of the Apostle Thomas?**

a. Carpenter
b. Merchant
c. Shepherd
d. Fisherman

8 **The largest surviving church of ancient times was built between 532 and 537. What is its name?**

a. Hagia Sophia
b. St Peter's
c. St John Lateran
d. St Justinian's

9 **On which psalm is the hymn 'All people that on earth do dwell' based?**

a. Psalm 14
b. Psalm 24
c. Psalm 100
d. Psalm 76

10 **Who wrote the poem 'The Windhover: to Christ our Lord'?**

a. George Herbert
b. T. S. Eliot
c. John Betjeman
d. Gerard Manley Hopkins

# THE WORLD OF THE BIBLE

1 By what other name is Mount Sinai known?

2 Why did Gehenna, a valley outside the city of Jerusalem, become another name for Hell?

3 From which mountain did Moses eventually see the Promised Land?

4 Judea lay within the bounds of which ancient empire during Jesus' lifetime?

5 In 2 Kings and Jeremiah we are told how King Zedekiah and many of the people of Judah were forced into exile. Where?

6 When Paul left Caesarea for Rome he suffered a tempestuous sea voyage which ended in shipwreck. Where did Paul and his companions find themselves?

7 Where did Elijah's famous contest take place with the priests of Baal to see whose god would ignite the altar?

8 Jesus's birth-place, Bethlehem, had another name. What was it?

9 In Jerusalem there is one location thought to be where Abraham made ready to sacrifice Isaac, where Solomon built his Temple and where Muhammad rose into heaven. Where is this?

10 When Jesus passed through Samaria near the town of Sychar, he paused by a well to talk to a Samaritan woman. What was the well called?

# CROSS SECTION

1 **Who was the Jewish High Priest to whom Jesus was first brought after his arrest?**
a. Annas
b. Caiaphas
c. Josephus
d. Philemon

2 **Which of these appears as the symbol for the World Council of Churches beneath the Greek word *OIKOYMENE?***
a. A book
b. A dove
c. A ship
d. A shepherd's crook

3 **Which of Jesus' ancestors is often depicted on his back asleep, or having a vision of the future, while a genealogical tree grows from him?**
a. Abraham
b. Noah
c. Jesse
d. Moses

4 **Which Old Testament king received the fatal message *'Mene, mene, tekel, upharsin'* which gave rise to the expression 'The writing on the wall'?**
a. David
b. Nebuchadnezzar
c. Solomon
d. Belshazzar

5 **On which day after his entry into Jerusalem did Christ rise from the tomb?**
a. Seventh
b. Eighth
c. Ninth
d. Tenth

6 **Where did Jesus perform the miracle of turning water into wine?**
a. Cana
b. Samaria
c. Capernaum
d. Tiberias

7 **Who was the second pope?**
a. Alexander
b. Clement
c. Sixtus I
d. Linus

8 **According to the Gospels of Mark and Luke what crime had Barabbas committed?**
a. Military desertion
b. Counterfeiting
c. Insurrection
d. Murder

9 **Who created the sculpture of St Michael victorious over the dragon on the rebuilt Coventry Cathedral?**
a. Jacob Epstein
b. Henry Moore
c. Barbara Hepworth
d. Ben Nicholson

10 **Which association did George Williams found in London in 1844?**
a. YMCA
b. USPG
c. YWCA
d. UMCA

# CRUSADES

1 Why were crusaders so called?

2 The First Crusade (1096-99) succeeded in winning back Jerusalem from which occupying force?

3 How many crusades to the Holy Land are there generally reckoned to have been?

4 In the early thirteenth century Pope Innocent III proclaimed a crusade against which European heretics?

5 Which early thirteenth-century crusade is believed to have been the source for the story of the Pied Piper of Hamelin?

6. In 1187 Saladin seized Jerusalem, prompting the Third Crusade. Which English king became one of its leaders?

7 A part monastic, part chivalric order of, formed in the twelfth century to protect pilgrims on the road to Palestine, had its headquarters in the Temple compound in Jerusalem. What was it called?

8 Another order successfully withstood a four-month siege of Malta by the Turks led by Suleiman in 1565. Who were they?

9 In Germany in particular, before Hitler's persecution, there occurred what Jews now called the First Holocaust. What was this?

10 When Constantinople was sacked during the Fourth Crusade in 1204, the venerated 'Image of Edessa' disappeared, possibly taken as booty. As what may it have reappeared?

# CROSS SECTION

1 **What is the name of the magazine distributed by the Worldwide Church of God?**
a. *The Plain Truth*
b. *Today's Church Today*
c. *Radio Church of God*
d. *Ten Lost Tribes*

2 **At which shrine in Ireland did Pope John Paul II pray on the centenary of the vision which gave rise to its becoming a place of pilgrimage?**
a. Blarney
b. Knock
c. Kells
d. Limerick

3 **Onto which part of Esau's body was Jacob holding when he was born?**
a. Hand
b. Arm
c. Heel
d. Ear

4 **From which tree is frankincense derived?**
a. Cedar
b. Olive
c. Balsam
d. Chestnut

5 **Why are eagles often depicted on lecterns?**
a. As symbols of divine wisdom
d. To ward off false prophets
c. As symbols of the Holy Spirit
d. To represent the victory of Christianity over the pagan eagle of the Roman empire

6 **In which country was the Council of Trent held in 1545-63?**
a. England
b. Austria
c. France
d. Spain

7 **Where was Eli priest in charge of the shrine?**

a. Shiloh
b. Jezreel
c. Ekron
d. Taanach

8 **As well as being the father of the Church of the New Jerusalem, he was also known as the father of 'crystallography' as a result of his scientific studies. What was his name?**

a. Emanuel Swedenborg
b John Gibson Paton
c James Legge
d Erik Erikson

9 **The foundation stone of which great religious building was laid by Pope Julius II in 1506?**

a. St John Lateran
b. St Peter's, Rome
c. The Duomo in Florence
d. The Leaning Tower of Pisa

10 **Who was the father of St James the Great and St John the Apostle?**

a. Zacharius
b. Zebedee
c. Levi
d. Ishmael

# BORN AGAIN

1 Whose early sermon and exhortation,'Repent, and be baptized every one of you in the name of Jesus Christ for the forgiveness of your sins' resulted in the conversion of about 'three thousand souls'?

2 A cartoonist and creator of Charlie Brown, Snoopy and Linus, converted from Lutheranism to the Church of God. Who is he?

3 According to St John's Gospel, who was urged by Jesus to be 'born anew'?

4 How old was Billy Graham when he experienced his conversion at a revival meeting led by Mordecai Ham?

5 For how long was Paul without sight after his conversion on the road to Damascus and who restored it to him?

6 Whose use of the 'anxious bench' is thought to have led to the practice of those seeking salvation coming to the front of the congregation at the end of evangelistic gatherings?

7 Bob Dylan and Cliff Richard are both notable converts to Christianity from the rock world. Which of them remained a Christian?

8 Who earned the rather scathing name of 'Holy Rollers' as a result of their ecstatic behaviour?

9 What is the modern nickname given to the use of the broadcasting media to evangelize and exhort?

10 Where do we find the words,'Seeing now, dearly beloved brethren, that these persons are regenerate'?

# CROSS SECTION

1 **Why did the Tower of Babel remain unfinished?**
a. The builders ran out of materials
b. The builders were taken into slavery
c. The builders suddenly began speaking in different languages
d. The builders died of a plague and could not be replaced

2 **How long were 'all the days of Methuselah'?**
a. 1001
b. 969
c. 666
d. 777

3 **At which university did the martyr John Huss teach?**
a. Prague
b. Bologna
c. Paris
d. Salzburg

4 **At which end of a church or cathedral is a rose window usually placed?**
a. West
b. North
c. South
d. East

5 **Which saint is symbolized by gold arrows on a red background?**
a. St Anthony
b. St Jude
c. St Lucy
d. St Sebastian

6 **When Jesus cured Bartimaeus, of what affliction was he healed?**
a. Leprosy
b. Paralysis
c. Blindness
d. Deafness

7 **Which is the largest cathedral in the British Isles?**
a. Liverpool
b. Guildford
c. Norwich
d. Durham

8 **Which British monarch was given the title Defender of the Faith by Pope Leo X?**
a. Henry VIII
b. Mary
c. James II
d. Anne

9 **Who was Noah's second son?**
a. Ham
b. Seth
c. Japheth
d. Cush

10 **To which European city did the first Baptists flee from persecution in England?**
a. Hamburg
b. Cologne
c. Amsterdam
d. Bruges

# MARTYRS REMEMBERED

1 Shakespeare wrote 'for Oldcastle died a martyr' *(Henry IV, Part 2* Epilogue*)*. Who was Sir John Oldcastle?

2 Who is regarded as being the first Christian martyr?

3 What fate was suffered by Christians condemned by the Roman authorities *'ad leonem'*?

4 Father Jerzy Popielusko was murdered in October 1984 by the secret police of which country?

5 Who wrote a *Book of Martyrs*, as it was popularly known, giving a history of English Protestant martyrs from the fourteenth to the sixteenth centuries?

6 During the reign of which Roman emperor do St Clement of Rome and later tradition say Sts Peter and Paul were put to death?

7 In 1900 a nationalist rebellion in China resulted in the death of European missionaries and thousands of Chinese converts. By what name is the rebellion known?

8 To which martyr's shrine are the pilgrims travelling in Chaucer's *Canterbury Tales*?

9 Who were canonized by the Roman Catholic Church in 1964, to become the first African saints?

10 Which Protestant martyrs are commemorated by the Martyrs Memorial in St Giles, Oxford?

# CROSS SECTION

1 **According to legend, which Irish monk sailed westwards from County Kerry and discovered a beautiful land, possibly part of North America?**
   a. St Brendan
   b. St Michael
   c. St Patrick
   d. St Columba

2 **Which of these words might also be used to describe a halo?**
   a. Aumbry
   b. Rubric
   c. Chrism
   d. Nimbus

3 **To whom did Salome present the head of John the Baptist?**
   a. Herod
   b. Pontius Pilate
   c. Herodias
   d. Philip

4 **What was the name of the priest who took a horn of oil out of the tabernacle and anointed Solomon at his coronation?**
   a. Abishag
   b. Adonijah
   c. Nathan
   d. Zadok

5 **How many priests marched around the walls of Jericho with the Ark of the Covenant, blowing on rams horns until the walls fell down?**
   a. 20
   b. 7
   c. 12
   d. 9

6 **What is the name of the sixteeth-century cathedral which stands in Moscow's Red Square?**

a. St Andrew's
b. St Nicholas'
c. St Basil's
d. St Peter's

7 **In which of his Epistles does St Paul write 'For the wages of sin is death'?**

a. Romans
b. Philippians
c. Ephesians
d. Colossians

8 **Where did Jesus cure the paralytic with the words,'Take up thy bed, and walk'?**

a. By the River Jordan
b. By the Sea of Galilee
c. By the pool named Bethesda
d. By the Dead Sea

9 **Who composed *The Crucifixion* in 1893?**

a. John Stainer
b. Gustav Holst
c. Arthur Sullivan
d. Joseph Barnby

10 **Which day is St Swithin's Day?**

a. 15 June
b. 21 June
c. 15 July
d. 21 July

# CHRISTIANITY GOES TO HOLLYWOOD

1 Charlton Heston played Moses in Cecil B. de Mille's 1956 version of *The Ten Commandments.* Who played the Pharaoh?

2 Which actress starred in the film *The Nun's Story*?

3 Who was Hollywood's 'Beautiful Hunk of Male', 'Mr Beefcake' and 'He-Man of the Year', and also Samson in de Mille's *Samson and Delilah*?

4 Who played both Christ in *The Greatest Story Ever Told* and a Jesuit priest in *The Exorcist*?

5 *The Bible* was conceived as a nine-hour extravaganza 'film of the Book'. When John Huston made the film in 1966 how much of the Bible did it contain?

6 Which Scottish athlete and missionary, known as 'The Flying Scotsman', who refused to take part in the qualifying heats of the 100 metres race in the 1924 Olympics, because they were run on a Sunday, features in the film *Chariots of Fire*?

7 In 1964 Pasolini released a film with which Gospel featuring in the title?

8 In 1943 Jennifer Jones made her film debut as Bernadette in *The Song of Bernadette*. Linda Darnell, better known as Chihuahua the saloon girl in *My Darling Clementine* and for other *femme fatale* roles, played who?

9 Bing Crosby, Pat O'Brien, and Spencer Tracy have one ecclesiastical thing in common. What is it?

10 Claude Rains played an angel in *Here Comes Mr Jordan.* Who did he play in *Angel on My Shoulder*?

# CROSS SECTION

1 **Who was Moses' brother?**
   a. Aaron
   b. Esau
   c. Hosea
   d. Zecariah

2 **Which Spanish city became, at about 1095, the centre for the Christian movement against the Moslem rulers of Spain?**
   a. Barcelona
   b. Toledo
   c. Granada
   d. Santiago de Compostela

3 **What is the name given to the bell tower detached from churches and cathedrals which originated in Italy, one of the most famous of which is the Leaning Tower of Pisa?**
   a. Duomo
   b. Angelus
   c. Pastoralia
   d. Campanile

4 **In which country did Eivind Berggrav take an active part in leading his native church to resist the Nazi occupation?**
   a. Denmark
   b. Norway
   c. Ukraine
   d. Hungary

5 **Where does the pope have his summer residence?**
   a. Fiesole
   b. Castel Gandolfo
   c. San Marino
   d. San Remo

6 **Which bishop fixed his see at Lichfield?**
   a. St Offa
   b. St Chad
   c. St Wilfrid
   d. St Osric

7 **From whom do the Malabar Christians of south-west India claim their origins?**
   a. St Jude
   b. St Stephen
   c. St Thomas the Apostle
   d. Joseph of Arimathea

8 **Which sect of American origin was founded under the name of International Bible Students?**
   a. Jehovah's Witnesses
   b. Disciples of Christ
   c. Anabaptists
   d. Free Presbyterians

9 **Which was the highest of the nine orders of angels?**
   a. Seraphim
   b. Powers
   c. Thrones
   d. Cherubim

10 **One of the extreme limits of Easter in the Western Church is 21 March, when is the other?**
   a. 25 April
   b. 21 April
   c. 30 April
   d. 15 April

# ALL GOD'S PEOPLE

1 Which Jewish sect, with its origins in first-century Palestine, rose to become another of the world's great religions?

2 St Pachomius, converted whilst a soldier in the Roman army in the fourth century, started one of the earliest Christian monastic communities among which ethnic group?

3 In the late twelfth century a rich merchant of Lyons in France, named Waldo, renounced his wealth and founded a sect that was eventually the target of a crusade in 1209 and other persections. What was the sect called?

4 Into which two groups did the Plymouth Brethren split after 1845?

5 Which monastic rule, dating from the sixth century, has provided the basis for most subsequent monastic life in the Western Church?

6 What was the name of the angel said by Joseph Smith to have revealed to him writings on golden plates which Smith translated and published as the Book of Mormon?

7 What is the meaning of the Latin word *nonna*, from which the word 'nun' is derived?

8 Which sect was taken to North America in 1774 by the wife of a Manchester blacksmith?

9 On which Hebridean island did St Columba found a monastery?

10 Before becoming known as Gordon of Khartoum, Charles George Gordon earned the sobriquet 'Chinese Gordon'. What was the name of the puritanical Christian rebellion in China which he helped suppress?

# CROSS SECTION

1 **The nave of Westminster Abbey was completed in 1163, but when were its western towers added?**
   a. 1740-50
   b. 1320-50
   c. 1470-20
   d. 1550-70

2 **Who designed the parade uniforms of the Papal Swiss Guard?**
   a. Pope John XVI
   b. Pope Innocent IV
   c. Michelangelo
   d. Raphael

3 **What was the occupation of the second son of Adam and Eve?**
   a. Shepherd
   b. Fruit farmer
   c. Priest
   d. Forester

4 **To which saint is York Minster dedicated**
   a. St Michael
   b. St Stephen
   c. St Peter
   d. St Luke

5 **Who was the only Englishman ever to occupy the see of Peter?**
   a. Nicholas III
   b. Hadarin VIII
   c. John II
   d. Hadrian IV

6 **How does a Greek cross differ from a Latin cross?**
   a. There are two transverse branches
   b. All the arms are of equal length
   c. There are three transverse branches
   d. It is shaped like the letter 'T'

7 **In which US university did the Campus Crusade for Christ begin its work among students?**

a. Syracuse
b. University of California at Los Angeles
c. Princeton
d. Harvard

8 **In 1938 she published the story of her life under the title *From Union Square to Rome:* she was also co-publisher of the newspaper *Catholic Worker.* What was her name?**

a. Dorothy Day
b. Frances Trollope
c. Mary Chesnut
d. Lydia Child

9 **To what religious use would you put a pricket?**

a. Fixing votive candles
b. Pouring away baptismal water
c. Securing the priests' vestments
d. Securing bell ropes

10 **How long was a cubit?**

a. 100 cm
b. 45 cm
c. 20 cm
d. 65 cm

# CRIES OF THE OPPRESSED

1 The emperor Diocletian instigated a time of severe persecution of Christians in 303, burning Scriptures, closing churches, imprisoning clergy and subjecting victims to torture and persecution. Which emperor ended this terror?

2 At Speke Hall near Liverpool, Chingle Hall, Lancashire, and in many other old houses there are confined spaces where persecuted clergy were concealed. What are such hiding places called?

3 In what part of the New World did Roger Williams, author of *The Bloody Tenent of Persecution* (1644), found a colony where freedom of religious worship was defined as a human right in its charter?

4 The third Monday in January is a public holiday in the USA. Which civil rights leader is commemorated by this?

5 Which South American work published in 1971 inspired and made famous Third-World liberation theology?

6 Julian of Norwich, Mother Ann (founder of the Shakers) and Mary Baker Eddy all anticipated feminist an aspect of theology in the way they thought of and addressed the Deity. How was this?

7 Liberation theology utilizes the political analysis of which secular philosophy?

8 Harriet Beecher Stowe published a novel in response to the Fugitive Slave Law in America in 1852 that was to become an international bestseller. What was it called?

9 What is the euphemism used to describe the victims of South American political regimes such as Pinochet's Chile and that of the junta in Argentina?

10 In the first two centuries AD, the Jews of Jerusalem rebelled against Rome on more than one occasion until finally the city was levelled, an altar to Jupiter put on the Temple site and the Jews banished. What was the name of the scattered Jewish population?

# CROSS SECTION

1 **Who was the pioneer missionary to Hawaii, whose work in the islands began in 1820?**
   a. William Passavant
   b. Hiram Bingham
   c. William Cunningham
   d. John Hamilton

2 **Which principal difference in the early English Church was settled by the Synod of Whitby in 663-4?**
   a. Date of Easter
   b. Date of Christmas
   c. Ownership of church lands
   d. Language of the holy Scriptures

3 **Who founded the Little Gidding community in 1625?**
   a. William Laud
   b. George Herbert
   c. Nathaniel Crashaw
   d. Nicholas Ferrar

4 **Which Bishop of Oxford attacked Darwin's theory of evolution in 1859, precipitating the later nineteenth-century conflict between science and religion?**
   a. Henry Manning
   b. Charles Spurgeon
   c. Samuel Wilberforce
   d. Thomas Huxley

5 **Which day in the Christian calendar is sometimes called Spy Wednesday?**
   a. Ash Wednesday
   b. First Wednesday after Christmas
   c. Wednesday before Good Friday
   d. First Wednesday in Advent

6 **Which Hebrew word translates as 'praise ye Yah(weh)'?**
   a. Alleluia
   b. Amen
   c. Kyrie
   d. Hosanna

7 **Which episode in the life of Christ is commemorated on 2 February?**

a. Sermon on the Mount
b. Naming of Jesus
c. Baptism of Jesus
d. Presentation of Christ in the Temple

8 **To whom were attributed the words 'Lord, make us instruments of your peace. Where there is hatred let us sow love'?**

a. Thomas Aquinas
b. Francis of Assisi
c. Abraham Lincoln
d. Joan of Arc

9 **Who called the Council of Nicea, which led to the promulgation of the Nicene Creed?**

a. Emperor Constantine
b. St Gregory
c. St Julius
d. St Benedict

10 **Where was the first Anglican church in North America built?**

a. New Amsterdam
b. Quebec
c. Jamestown
d. Newport

# DUST TO DUST

1 At the beginning of the Order for the Burial of the Dead there is a note that the office is not to be used in certain cases. What are they?

2 Which churchyard was made famous by Thomas Gray in his *Elegy in a Country Churchyard*?

3 In whose tomb was Jesus' body laid?

4 According to legend, the occupant of a large grave in Hathersage churchyard, Derbyshire, chose the spot by shooting an arrow and watching where it fell. Who was he?

5 The parish church at Odiham, Hampshire, has a 'pesthouse' in its graveyard. What was it used for?

6 Which London cemetery is well known both for the fantastic designs of many of the tombs and for the famous people buried there, among them George Eliot and Christina Rossetti?

7 For how long had Lazarus of Bethany been lying in his tomb before Jesus raised him?

8 In Much Marcle churchyard in Herefordshire there is a tree that seats eight people inside its hollowed out trunk and in the churchyard at Stoke Gabriel, Devon there is one said to be 1500 years old. What kind of tree are both of these?

9 Dr Francis Douce of Nether Wallop, Hampshire had a structure fifteen feet high built to serve as his memorial in the churchyard. What is it?

10 In which cemetery is this epitaph reputed to be found?

*Played five aces*
*Now playing the harp*

# CROSS SECTION

1 **Who sought 'to justify the ways of God to man'?**
   a. Christina Rossetti
   b. Andrew Marvell
   c. William Shakespeare
   d. John Milton

2 **The 1910 conference in which city led to the establishment of the International Missionary Council?**
   a. Edinburgh
   b. Toronto
   c. Exeter
   d. Geneva

3 **Which of these is the odd one out?**
   a. Reginald Fitz-Urse
   b. Thomas à Becket
   c. William de Tracy
   d. Hugh de Morville

4 **What is the name of the deaconess of the Church at Cenchreae, mentioned in Romans 16.1?**
   a. Phoebe
   b. Rachel
   c. Ruth
   d. Catherine

5 **What is the paten used for in Christian services?**
   a. Holding bread at the celebration of the Eucharist
   b. Holding baptismal water
   c. Supporting holy Scriptures
   d. Extinguishing altar candles

6 **Where was the lengendary medieval monarch, Prester John, believed to have been king?**
   a. Atlantis
   b. Asia
   c. China
   d. Russia

7 **Who is Ras Tafari to his followers?**
 a. Emperor Haile Selassie
 b. Marcus Garvie
 c. Solomon
 d. Adam

8 **By what name is the Children's Special Service Mission, founded in 1867, now known?**
 a. United Society for the Propagation of the Gospel
 b. Scripture Union
 c. Boys Brigade
 d. Christian Aid

9 **Which English composer wrote the motet *Spem in Alium* for eight choirs of five parts each?**
 a. Benjamin Britten
 b. Edward Elgar
 c. Thomas Tallis
 d. William Byrd

10 **Which of the following is popularly known as the 'Wee Frees'?**
 a. United Free Church of Scotland
 b. Free Methodists
 c. Free Unitarian Church
 d. Free Church of Scotland

# ONWARD CHRISTIAN WOMEN

1 Who asks,'Judge for yourselves; is it proper for a woman to pray to God with her head uncovered'?

2 What do the initials WCTU stand for?

3 When did the Church of England decide to ordain women to the priesthood?

4 Who is the patron saint of good housewives?

5 Which author, known chiefly for her murder mysteries, is also highly regarded for writings and plays with strongly Christian themes?

6 What was the name of the 'queen' of gospel music who sang at President Kennedy's inauguration, before Martin Luther King's 'I have a dream' speech and a few years later at his funeral?

7 Who was known as 'The Holy Maid of Kent' and was hanged at Tyburn in 1534 for denouncing Henry VIII's divorce and remarriage to Anne Boleyn?

8 What was the first name of William Booth's wife, with whom he founded what was to become known as the Salvation Army?

9 In the Yorkshire Dales one can now go on the Lady Anne Clifford trail. For what was this seventeenth-century benefactoress chiefly known?

10 Who wrote, 'Much depends on the spirit in which the visitor enters upon her work. It must be the spirit, not of judgement, but of mercy. She must not say in her heart, I am more holy than thou'?

# CROSS SECTION

1 **To whom did Jesus give the name Boanerges?**
  a. The sons of Zebedee
  b. The Pharisees
  c. All his disciples
  d. The moneylenders in the Temple

2 **In which country was Job's home?**
  a. Dan
  b. Uz
  c. Zoba
  d. Maspha

3 **In which city are the relics of 'Good King Wenceslas' enshrined?**
  a. Rouen
  b. Pisa
  c. Vienna
  d. Prague

4 **Who wrote the hymn 'Onward Christian Soldiers'?**
  a. Sabine Baring-Gould
  b. Isaac Watts
  c. Reginald Heber
  d. John Newton

5 **Where did the Baptist Missionary Society send its first missionary in 1793?**
  a. Jamaica
  b. China
  c. India
  d. Congo

6 **Of whom does David say 'How are the mighty fallen . . .'?**
  a. Amelekites
  b. Saul and Jonathan
  c. Jezreelites
  d. Hadadezer and the Syrians

7 **In which of these places does Eastern Orthodox rule forbid access to both women and female animals?**
a. Mount Olympus
b. Mount Athos
c. Mount of Olives
d. Mount Carmel

8 **What distinguished the stylites from other Christians?**
a. They lived on the tops of pillars
b. They lived alone on isolated islands
c. They lived in pits in the ground
d. They lived in caves

9 **Which biblical event traditionally took place on Karn Hattin?**
a. Sermon on the Mount
b. Elijah's ascent into heaven
c. David's victory over Goliath
d. Jesus' encounter with Satan

10 **In which Latin American country was Archbishop Oscar Romero assassinated in 1980?**
a. El Salvador
b. Guatemala
c. Nicaragua
d. Colombia

# SONGS OF PRAISE

1 Which poet wrote the words of 'In the bleak midwinter . . . '?

2 In which year was Hymns, Ancient and Modern published?

3 Who wrote the popular hymn 'Servant King'?

4 Which Christmas hymn, sung by Bing Crosby in The Bells of St Mary's, was hastily composed on Christmas Eve in 1818 to be accompanied on the guitar, after the church organ broke down in Oberndorf, in Austria?

5 Who wrote, among 400 other hymns, 'All things bright and beautiful', 'Once in royal David's city' and 'There is a green hill far away'?

6 From which American sect came the hymn 'Tis the gift to be simple, 'tis the gift to be free'?

7 'Abide with me' was written by Henry Francis Lyte. On which biblical story is it said to have been based?

8 Augustus Montague Toplady, the eighteenth-century clergyman and hymn writer, is said to have written a particularly famous hymn while visiting Cheddar Gorge in Somerset. What was it?

9 Who wrote 'The Lord of the Dance'?

10 And who wrote?

*Sing on, with hymns uproarious,*
*Ye humble and aloof,*
*Look up! and oh how glorious*
*He has restored the roof!*

# CROSS SECTION

1 **Where does the controversial London Church of Christ have its international headquarters?**

a. Birmingham
b. Los Angeles
c. Vancouver
d. Amsterdam

2 **Where were the bones of the Venerable Bede 'translated' to in the eleventh century?**

a. York
b. Lincoln
c. Durham
d. Hexham

3 **How many Beatitudes are there?**

a. 6
b. 12
c. 10
d. 8

4 **In which Gospels do we find the words,'Ask, and it will be given you; seek, and you will find; knock and it will be opened to you'?**

a. Matthew
b. Mark
c. Luke
d. John

5 **In which year did the House of Commons reject a new Prayer Book by a majority of 266 to 220?**

a. 1876
b. 1977
c. 1912
d. 1928

6 **When the Lutheran and Reformed Churches in Prussia united in 1817 what was the official name given to the new Church they formed?**

a. Evangelical Church
b. Reformed Lutheran Church
c. New Lutheran Church
d. Prussian Free Church

7 **Which is the smallest cathedral in England?**

a. Truro
b. Carlisle
c. Oxford
d. Chester

8 **When is the feast of St Michael and All Angels?**

a. 29 July
b. 29 August
c. 29 September
d. 29 October

9 **How many 'last words' did Jesus speak from the cross?**

a. 39
b. 15
c. 12
d. 7

10 **On which finger of the monarch's hand does the Archbishop of Canterbury place the 'Coronation Ring'?**

a. Second finger of the left hand
b. Third finger of the left hand
c. Fourth finger of the right hand
d. Third finger of the right hand

## HOLY WRIT: THE BIBLE ANCIENT AND MODERN

1 Where does the word 'Bible' come from?

2 What are the three original languages of the Bible?

3 What is the name of the settlement near to which the Dead Sea Scrolls were found hidden in a cave?

4 What was the Vulgate Bible?

5 Where was Tyndale's English New Testament printed in 1526?

6 What year saw the publication of the King James' version of the Bible?

7 Why, before the Revolution, was the publication of an English Bible prohibited in America?

8 What was the 'Ears to Ear Bible'?

9 Which compiler of a famous American dictionary also published a version of the Bible in 1833 with British spelling and archaic language removed?

10 What was the 'Mite Bible'?

# CROSS SECTION

1 **Which of these is an old name for Maundy Thursday?**
   a. Sheer Thursday
   b. Penny Thursday
   c. Penance Thursday
   c. Good Thursday

2 **In 1954 Martin Luther King became a minister in a church in which state?**
   a. Louisiana
   b. Alabama
   c. Iowa
   d. Illinois

3 **Which of these comes closest to the number of hymns written by Charles Wesley?**
   a. 3000
   b. 4000
   c. 2500
   d. 5500

4 **In which country did Archbishop Janani Luwum die while in the hands of security forces in 1977?**
   a. South Africa
   b. Angola
   c. Uganda
   d. Mozambique

5 **Which nineteenth-century monk is honoured as the 'apostle of Alaska'?**
   a. St Herman
   b. St Juneau
   c. St Aleutian
   d. St Albert

6 **What do Anglicans traditionally call the second Sunday in Advent?**
   a. Star Sunday
   b. Preparation Sunday
   c. Bible Sunday
   d. Stir Up Sunday

**7 Which conference held in 1604 proposed the translation of the Bible that came to be known as 'King James' Bible'?**

a. Westminster Conference
b. Lambeth Conference
c. Hampton Court Conference
d. St James' Conference

**8 Who was St Augustine's mother?**

a. St Angela
b. St Matilda
c. St Agatha
d. St Monica

**9 In which of these ecclesiastical seasons does the Western Church use the colour violet?**

a. Ascension
b. Epiphany
c. Advent
d. Christmas

**10 What is Good Friday known as in the Greek Orthodox Church?**

a. Great Friday
b. Black Friday
c. Sad Friday
d. Lost Friday

# ACTS OF THE APOSTLES

1 To whom is the Acts of the Apostles addressed?

2 Who was the author of the Acts of the Apostles?

3 When 'a young man', Saul, first appears in Acts he is present at and 'consenting' to a terrible deed. What was it?

4 Which Apostle was Simon Peter's brother?

5 Who converted Simon, the magician practising in Samaria?

6 To whom did Peter say,'Stand up; I myself also am a man'?

7 What is the Apostolic succession?

8 What is the name of the place, mentioned at the beginning of Acts, where Christ gathered his Apostles to prepare them for his ascension?

9 In which city were Paul and Silas beaten and imprisoned for curing a slave-girl of her spirit of divination, so depriving her owners of revenue?

10 Which Apostle is said to have gone to Ephesus to live with and care for Mary, Jesus' mother?

# CROSS SECTION

1 **When does Ascension Day fall?**
  a. Fourth Wednesday after Easter
  b. Third Thursday after Easter
  c. Sixth Wednesday after Easter
  d. Fifth Thursday after Easter

2 **In the Church of Scotland, who does the Lord High Commissioner represent?**
  a. Sovereign
  b. Moderator
  c. Procurator
  d. Church of Scotland overseas

3 **In which year did the Evangelical Alliance of Great Britain first hold a universal week of prayer?**
  a. 1820
  b. 1846
  c. 1875
  d. 1893

4 **Who was the first Roman Catholic to be elected president of the United States?**
  a. John Kennedy
  b. Jimmy Carter
  c. Ronald Reagan
  d. Gerald Ford

5 **In which African country was the Church of Jesus Christ on Earth by the Prophet Simon Kimbangu, to give it its full name, founded?**
  a. Sudan
  b. Nigeria
  c. Zaire
  d. Sierra Leone

6 **Where did the World Council of Churches convene its first general assembly in 1948?**
  a. London
  b. Milan
  c. Athens
  d. Amsterdam

7 **What is ontology?**
  a. Study of angels
  b. Study of being
  c. Study of healing
  d. Study of teaching

8 **Who became Archbishop of Canterbury in 1928?**
  a. Cosmo Gordon Lang
  b. Frederick Temple
  c. William Temple
  d. Randall Thomas Davidson

9 **In which diocese was George Carey bishop immediately before he became Archbishop of Canterbury?**
  a. Bristol
  b. Bath and Wells
  c. Ely
  d. Lichfield

10 **An apple shown in the hands of Adam depicts sin, but what does it depict in the hands of Christ or the Blessed Virgin?**
  a. Salvation
  b. Penance
  c. Knowledge
  d. Generosity

# THE CHRISTIAN WORLD TODAY

1 In which country did the now international counselling organization Marriage Encounter have its origins?

2 Which body of the Church of England was established in 1958 'to promote and co-ordinate the thought and action of the Church in matters affecting man's life in society'?

3 For which group of people was the Metropolitan Church founded in America by Troy Perry?

4 Which missionary society was founded in 1934 by the American translator, Cameron Townsend?

5 Which leader from the old Communist world had a historic meeting with Pope John Paul II at the Vatican on 1 December 1989?

6 In 1982 an Anglican report on disarmament was published. What was it called?

7 In 1968 Pope Paul VI published an encyclical condemning artificial birth control, abortion and sterilization. What is it called?

8 What was the Archbishop's Commission on Rural Areas report, published in 1990, called?

9 Which archbishop was awarded the Nobel Peace Prize in 1984?

10 In 1984 the appointment of the new Bishop of Durham led to some controversy because of his views on the symbolic rather than the literal truth of certain stories in the Bible. What was the bishop's name?

# CROSS SECTION

1 **How many Deadly Sins are there?**
   a. 6
   b. 8
   c. 10
   d. 7

2 **What is the name of America's largest black Pentecostal church, founded by Charles Mason and renowned for its gospel music?**
   a. Christ Universal Temple
   b. Church of God in Christ
   c. Assemblies of God
   d. Dexter Avenue Baptist Church

3 **With whom does the Bible say Jacob wrestled all night beside a stream?**
   a. An angel
   b. The devil
   c. A man
   d. A lion

4 **What was the name of the first Holy Roman Emperor, whose shrine is in Aachen Cathedral?**
   a. Charlemagne
   b. St Peter
   c. Roland
   d. Tiberius

5 **Who is believed to have planted a staff on Wearyall Hill that grew into the Glastonbury Thorn?**
   a. King Arthur
   b. St Paul
   c. Joseph of Arimathea
   d. St Augustine

6 **What was the name given by early Christians to their Love Feast?**
   a. Philia
   b. Agape
   c. Eros
   d. Caritas

7 **What was the Molten Sea?**

a. The fiery lake in Hell
b. The Red Sea
c. A huge bronze bowl in the precincts of Solomon's Temple
d. A huge bowl in which gold was melted to make the golden calf

8 **Which Sunday is Mothering Sunday?**

a. The Feast of the Virgin Mary
b. The fourth Sunday in Lent
c. The first Sunday after Easter
d. The Purification of St Mary the Virgin

9 **What is the name given to the social ostracism of one who is an unrepentent sinner, practised especially in the Mennonite and Amish communities?**

a. Shunning
b. Casting Out
c. Avoidance
d. Banishment

10 **What title does the Patriarch of the Armenian Church carry?**

a. Archbishop
b. Catholicos
c. Dominus
d. Papa

# FATHER BROWN AND FRIENDS

1 In which novel did G.K. Chesterton first introduce his priest-cum-detective, Father Brown, to the public?

2 Upon whom does Samuel Butler base his unflattering portrait of Theobald Pontifex, the Rector of Battersby-on-the-Hill, in *The Way of All Flesh*?

3 What is the name of Oliver Goldsmith's Vicar of Wakefield?

4 How is Umberto Eco's fourteenth-century Franciscan detective linked to Conan Doyle's nineteenth-century London detective?

5 Who created this character?

> *. . . being much given to describe himself, both verbally and in writing, as a vessel, he is occasionally mistaken by strangers for a gentleman connected with navigation; but, he is, as he expresses it, 'in the ministry'.*

6. In Trollope's *Barchester Towers*, who is the Bishop of Barchester?

7 Which of Jane Austen's characters in *Mansfield Park* is saying this to Edmund Bertram with an arch smile: 'I am just as much surprised now as I was at first that you should intend to take orders. You really are fit for something better'?

8 In which of Henry Fielding's novels do we meet the amiable Parson Adams?

9 Who wrote *Scenes of Clerical Life*, published in 1858?

10 To which country did Graham Greene's visit inspire his novel *The Power and the Glory* with its flawed hero, a Catholic priest persecuted by the authorities?

# CROSS SECTION

1 **According to the doctrine of Nestorianism, how many separate Persons were there in the incarnate Christ?**
  a. 3
  b. 4
  c. 2
  d. 5

2 **Who in Genesis said,'This now is bone of my bone, and flesh of my flesh'?**
  a. Cain
  b. Enoch
  c. Adam
  d. Noah

3 **Why did God smite Uzzah when David was bringing the Ark of the Covenant to Jerusalem?**
  a. Because he was not a Jew
  b. Because he touched the Ark
  c. Because he blasphemed
  d. Because he killed one of those carrying it

4 **What is Take Six?**
  a. A group of black gospel singers
  b. A Charismatic Church founded in 1976
  c. A Christian counselling service
  d. A take-away restaurant in London, run by Christians

5 **What was distinctive about Rechabites?**
  a. They abstained from alcoholic drink
  b. They did not eat meat
  c. They did not drink milk
  d. They could only eat bread made from the gleanings of the harvest

6 **What is another name for the Star of David?**
  a. The Zionist Star
  b. The Star of Bethlehem
  c. Blaze
  d. Solomon's Seal

7 **How many canonical hours are there in the Divine Office?**
a. 9
b. 11
c. 7
d. 12

8 **Whose reported last words were these,'We shall this day light a candle by God's grace in England, as I trust never shall be put out'?**
a. Ridley's
b. Latimer's
c. Cranmer's
d. Archbishop Laud's

9 **Dorcas, a woman well known for her charitable acts, was raised by Peter from the dead when he visited which city?**
a. Damascus
b. Jerusalem
c. Caesarea
d. Joppa

10 **What does the name 'Immanuel' mean?**
a. Praise be to God
b. God shall triumph
c. God with us
d. Yahweh

# FOUR FOR THE GOSPEL MAKERS

1 Why is the Book of Numbers so called?

2 How many golden balls comprise the symbol of St Nicholas?

3 How many tribes of Israel were there?

4 In the parable of the wise and foolish virgins, how many were there all together?

5 How many pillars does 'Wisdom's' house have?

6 When Peter asks Jesus if he should forgive someone seven times, what is Jesus' reply?

7 How many sacraments do Protestant Churches have?

8 How many sacraments are there in the Roman Catholic Church?

9 At what hour did Jesus die?

10 How many plagues of Egypt were there?

# CROSS SECTION

1 **What in medieval churches are the sedilia?**
  a. Stone seats set into the wall for the clergy
  b. Vessels used during Holy Communion
  c. A kind of vaulting
  d. Little supporting buttresses

2 **What does the name Pentecost mean when translated into English?**
  a. The fiftieth day
  b. Resurrection
  c. Ascension
  d. Five blessings

3 **What is another name for the Sea of Galilee?**
  a. Sea of Souls
  b. Sea of Life
  c. Sea of Tiberias
  d. Sea of Israel

4 **Which is the liturgical language used by Chaldean Christians?**
  a. Latin
  b. Greek
  c. Syriac
  d. Russian

5 **Which word is used to describe in theology the explanation of Biblical texts?**
  a. Exegesis
  b. Mimesis
  c. Thesis
  d. Explesis

6 **What does a Tau cross look like?**
  a. The letter 'X'
  b. A telegraph pole with three arms
  c. The letter 'T'
  d. A Maltese cross on a vertical stem

7 **To which of these places was the Syrian monk St Theodore of Tarsus sent from Rome in 667?**

a. Antioch
b. Bethlehem
c. Canterbury
d. Damascus

8 **In addition to the dove, Noah released another bird from the ark after it had come to rest on Mount Ararat. Which was it?**

a. Eagle
b. Raven
c. Swan
d. Duck

9 **Which word completes this quotation from Mark 9.24, 'Lord, I believe: help my . . .'?**

a. Faith
b. Knowledge
c. Prayer
d. Unbelief

10 **According to tradition, who pulled out the Holy Nails after Christ's crucifixion?**

a. Peter
b. A Roman centurion
c. Nicodemus
d. An angel

# THE POWER AND THE GLORY

1 Which Oxford College did Cardinal Wolsey establish?

2 Which king's wish to be rid of 'this turbulent priest' resulted in the murder of Thomas à Becket?

3 What was Pope Alexander VI's original name?

4 Of which political party is Ian Paisley the leader?

5 Which French prelate living in the sixteenth and seventeenth centuries virtually governed France, destroying the Huguenots, conducting military campaigns against Savoy and Spain, and establishing a web of intrigue and espionage to the chagrin of his enemies?

6 In which year was Pope John Paul II shot in St Peter's Square?

7 Who was both head of state and Archbishop of Cyprus in the 1960s and 1970s?

8 This Baptist minister founded Moral Majority Inc., wielded considerable influence with the voters in the 1980 and 1984 US presidential elections and was listed in one publication in 1982 as one of the the twenty most prominent Americans. What is his name?

9 In the late ninteeth and early twentieth centuries a 'mystic' and 'holy man' gained enormous power over the wife of the Tsar of Russia and eventually the court and state politics. His name was Grigoriy Efimovich but he earned a nickname which in English means 'dissolute'. What was it?

10 Which American Catholic priest conducted the first religious service to be televised, received an average of 40,000 letters a week from his viewers and was awarded an Emmy?

# CROSS SECTION

1 **The American Bible Society was founded in 1816 to promote the circulation and reading of the Bible, but how many Bible societies were there in the United States before 1816?**
   a. None
   b. 24
   c. 80
   d. 128

2 **After which date was Christianity made the only legal religion in the Roman Empire?**
   a. 385
   b. 444
   c. 400
   d. 576

3 **Which of the four Gospels did the early Christians regard as the most comprehensive and authoritative account of the life of Christ?**
   a. Matthew
   b. Mark
   c. Luke
   d. John

4 **When does the Orthodox Church celebrate 'the Triumph of Orthodoxy'?**
   a. First Sunday in Advent
   b. First Sunday in Lent
   c. Easter Sunday
   d. Ascension Day

5 **In which Italian city was Savonarola hanged in 1498?**
   a. Rome
   b. Milan
   c. Florence
   d. Venice

6 **In which of the books of the Old Testament is this prophesied 'But thou, Beth-lehem Ephratah, though thou be little among the thousands of Judah, yet out of thee shall he come forth unto me that is to be ruler in Israel'?**

a. Micah
b. Isaiah
c. Jeremiah
d. Hosea

7 **What nationality was the sixteenth-century religious reformer Ulrich Zwingli?**

a. Italian
b. German
c. Flemish
d. Swiss

8 **What was the first commandment given by God to the first humans of his creation?**

a. To be fruitful and multiply
b. Not to eat the forbidden fruit
c. To tend the Garden of Eden
d. To work for six days only and keep the seventh a day of rest

9 **Who were the Marranos who became victims of the Spanish Inquisition?**

a. Converts from Judaism
b. Converts from Islam
c. Converts from Protestantism
d. Lapsed Roman Catholics

10 **Two goats were chosen by lot on the Jewish Day of Atonement. The scapegoat was driven out into the wilderness with the sins of the people. What happened to the other goat?**

a. It was kept in the Temple
b. It was sacrificed
c. It was given to the Chief Priest
d. It was drowned to cleanse the people

# LET US PRAY: LORE AND LITURGY

1 In which year did the Church of England set up its Liturgical Commission?

2 What was the name of the French priest who became well known for his opposition to the liturgical reforms of the Second Vatican Council and who was eventually excommunicated by Pope John Paul II?

3 What is the derivation of the word 'Eucharist'?

4 'There was never anything by the wit of man so well devised, or so sure established, which in continuance hath not been corrupted . . . ' As what?

5 The Mass is divided into two liturgies. What are they?

6 During which century was the Nicene Creed composed?

7 Why is a Collect so called?

8 What is a Doxology?

9 What words follow the Absolution in the Book of Common Prayer (1662)?

10 The opening words of which New Testament Epistle form the Epistle for Christmas Day?

# CROSS SECTION

1 **Which angel is the leader of the group of angels known as Powers?**
   a. Gabriel
   b. Michael
   c. Raphael
   d. George

2 **In which religious tradition was Guy Fawkes, the most famous member of the 1605 Gunpowder Plot, brought up?**
   a. Roman Catholic
   b. Anglican
   c. Quaker
   d. Lutheran

3 **Which of Paul's epistles was written to the Church founded in a Roman colony that stood on the site of a battle which Shakespeare mentions in *Julius Caesar*?**
   a. Ephesians
   b. Titus
   c. Philippians
   d. Colossians

4 **Which of the four Gospels is the shortest?**
   a. Matthew
   b. Mark
   c. Luke
   d. John

5 **There is a traditional story that a woman called Veronica wiped sweat from Jesus' face when he stumbled under the weight of the cross. The cloth she used bore his image thereafter. Where is this relic now housed?**
   a. St Peter's, Rome
   b. The Church of the Holy Sepulchre
   c. Turin Cathedral
   d. Reims

6 **The Mesopotamian epic *Gilgamesh*, dating from at least 2000 BC, bears striking similarities to which Old Testament story?**
a. David and Goliath
b. Exodus
c. The Fall of Jericho
d. Noah and the Flood

7 **According to Luke's Gospel, where did Jesus' ascension take place?**
a. Mount of Olives
b. Bethany
c. Gethsemane
d. The Temple precincts

8 **To which ancient god were infant children sacrificed?**
a. Molech
b. Ishtar
c. Marduk
d. Asshur

9 **Which composer, born in the last century, composed a liturgy of Vespers and Matins referred to collectively as *All-Night Vigil*?**
a. Tchaikovsky
b. Elgar
c. Rachmaninoff
d. Bruckner

10 **Why did the name Abigail become synonymous with 'servant'?**
a. Because a St Abigail was renowned for acts of servitude
b. Because David's wife Abigail called herself his handmaid
c. It was the name of all unmarried Jewish girl servants
d. Abigail is Hebrew for 'servant'

# THE CHRISTIAN HERITAGE: CATHEDRALS

1 A Russian-born French artist, well known for his dream and fantasy-filled paintings, designed a stained glass window, inspired by Psalm 150, for Chichester Cathedral. What is the artist's name?

2 One of the most striking features of Wells Cathedral is the heavily proportioned strainer arches over the nave. What is the purpose of such arches?

3 Which European cathedral covers the largest area?

4 What lies beneath York Minster?

5 What famous event led to the construction of many of Sir Christopher Wren's greatest works including St Paul's Cathedral in London?

6 Who spent the last thirty years of his life working on the designs and building of St Peter's in Rome?

7 Who designed the extraordinary 'cathedral-temple' of the Holy Family in Barcelona, work on which has been in progress since the 1880s?

8 Which French Gothic cathedral is adorned by 130 beautiful windows and 2,200 stone figures?

9 Which architect was given the task of designing a new Coventry Cathedral after the wartime bombing of its predecessor?

10 Which cathedral is depicted on the Bayeux tapestry?

# CROSS SECTION

1 **Who owned the house in the street called Straight in which the Lord told Ananias to enquire 'for one called Saul, of Tarsus'?**

a. Judas
b. Timothy
c. Eli
d. Joseph

2 **What is the nationality of Emilio Castro, who in 1985 was elected General Secretary of the World Council of Churches?**

a. American
b. Portuguese
c. Uruguayan
d. Mexican

3 **In which year did Judge Bennett sentence George Fox to six months in prison, having derisively referred to Fox and his followers as 'quakers'?**

a. 1600
b. 1580
c. 1650
d. 1720

4 **By what name are members of what was originally the Christian Commercial Men's Association of America now known?**

a. Gideons
b. Uniates
c. Mormons
d. New Evangelicans

5 **Which book in the King James' Version of the Bible has the smallest number of words?**

a. Third Epistle of John
b. Haggai
c. Lamentations
d. Epistle of James

6 **What was the original name of the man who, according to Acts 5.36, 'by the apostles was surnamed Barnabas'?**
   a. Joses
   b. Peter
   c. Paul
   d. Jonathan

7 **Who was consecrated the first woman bishop of the Episcopal Church in America in 1989?**
   a. Revd Eve Stacey
   b. Revd Barbara Harris
   c. Revd Carole Hines
   d. Revd Mary Lucas

8 **In which style did the eighteenth-century ecclesiastical architects Balthasar Neumann, J. M. Fischer and Dom. Zimmermann work?**
   a. Gothic
   b. Neo-Classical
   c. Baroque
   d. Romanesque

9 **Who did Philipp Melanchthon follow as a theological leader in the sixteenth century?**
   a. Luther
   b. Torquemada
   c. Ignatius Loyola
   d. Teresa of Avila

10 **In which year did the Russian Orthodox Church mark its millennium?**
   a. 1950
   b. 1910
   c. 1988
   d. 1898

# OBERAMMERGAU TO THE OLD VIC: CHRISTIANITY ON THE STAGE

1 In medieval times, mystery plays were most frequently performed during which Church festival?

2 With whom is Everyman arguing in the fifteenth-century morality play of the same name?

3 What was the reason for the enactment of the Passion play at Oberammergau every ten years?

4 Who played the heroine of Shaw's *St Joan* in the first London production in 1924?

5 With whom did Andrew Lloyd Webber collaborate to produce *Joseph and the Amazing Technicolor Dreamcoat* and *Jesus Christ Superstar*?

6 Who played Sir Thomas More in Robert Bolt's play *A Man for all Seasons* when it was first produced in 1960?

7 Although in Goethe's *Faust* the legendary doctor has made his bargain with Mephistopheles, what happens to his soul at the end?

8 T. S. Eliot's play *Murder in the Cathedral* was written in 1935 for what occasion?

9 What was the title of Christopher Fry's play about St Cuthbert?

10 From which musical come the songs 'Day by Day' and 'Prepare Ye the Way of the Lord'?

# CROSS SECTION

1 **Where in Poland is the shrine of the Black Madonna which has long been a site of national pilgrimage?**
   a. Gdansk
   b. Cracow
   c. Szczecin
   d. Czestochowa

2 **Who regularly accompanied the evangelist Dwight Lyman Moody with singing and organ-playing?**
   a. Ira David Sankey
   b. Joel A. Carpenter
   c. Nathaniel William Turner
   d. Gerald B. Winrod

3 **What nationality was the theologian Karl Barth who published a famous commentary on Romans in 1919?**
   a. German
   b. Austrian
   c. Dutch
   d. Swiss

4 **Approximately how many years of Jewish history are spanned in the Bible by the books from Joshua to Esther?**
   a. 500
   b. 5000
   c. 800
   d. 1500

5 **Which village gave its name to the collection of hymns published in 1779 by the poet William Cowper and the converted slave-trader John Newton?**
   a. Osney
   b. Otterbury
   c. Ovington
   d. Olney

6 **With which event in Christ's life does St Mark open his Gospel?**

a. His birth
b. His baptism by John the Baptist
c. His death
d. His resurrection

7 **In which city were the followers of Jesus first called Christians?**

a. Tyre
b. Ephesus
c. Damascus
d. Antioch

8 **Which saint has the emblem of a silver lantern and a gold staff on a red background?**

a. St Jude
b. St Christopher
c. St Barnabas
d. St Leo

9 **Which building in Jerusalem stands on the site of Solomon's Temple?**

a. Church of the Holy Sepulchre
b. Dome of the Rock
c. Herod's tomb
d. Herod's palace

10 **To which Roman Catholic order did Leonardo Boff, one of the key figures in contemporary liberation theology, belong?**

a. Benedictine
b. Dominican
c. Franciscan
d. Carmelite

# WHO'S IN THE NEW TESTAMENT

1 Who were nicknamed 'the sons of thunder'?

2 The same high priest delivered Jesus to Pontius Pilate, sent letters to the synagogues when Saul was setting out for Damascus and, early legend says, later became a Christian. What was his name?

3 Why has one of the Marys in the New Testament the name Magdalene?

4 Who were Ananias and Sapphira?

5 In Acts and in the Epistles 1 Corinthians and Romans, we meet another Christian husband and wife team whose point of contact originally with Paul is the same trade of tentmaking. What are they called?

6 Which of the five members of the Herod family mentioned in the New Testament was responsible for John the Baptist's death?

7 Which Roman procurator held Paul in detention in Caesarea for two years, hoping for a ransom in exchange for Paul's release?

8 What was the name of the husband of Mary's kinswoman, Elizabeth?

9 How old was Anna the prophetess who recognized Jesus' unique qualities when she saw nim at the Temple?

10 To which of the Gospel writers was Jerome referring when he said,'Peter spoke, he wrote it down'?

# CROSS SECTION

1 **Who was Samuel's mother?**

a. Hannah
b. Elizabeth
c. Miriam
d. Kezia

2 **Which order of knights was destroyed in the early fourteenth century during the papacy of Clement V?**

a. Templars
b. Hospitallers
c. Knights of Malta
d. Knights of Rhodes

3 **Which animals ate the body of Jezebel, according to 2 Kings 9.36?**

a. Wolves
b. Rats
c. Dogs
d. Lions

4 **In which city was Zacchaeus a tax collector?**

a. Bethlehem
b. Gaza
c. Jericho
d. Damascus

5 **Which of the twelve Apostles pointed out to Jesus the boy with five loaves and two fishes?**

a. James
b. John
c. Simon
d. Andrew

6 **Who was responsible for making the golden calf which the Israelites worshipped when Moses was on Mount Sinai?**

a. Joseph
b. Levi
c. Eli
d. Aaron

7 **'Congress shall make no law respecting an establishment of religion or prohibiting the free exercise thereof.' Which Amendment to the US Constitution is this?**

a. First
b. Second
c. Third
d. Fourth

8 **Who wrote the poem *The Dream of Gerontius* in 1865?**

a. Cardinal Newman
b. Cardinal Manning
c. Cardinal Vaughan
d. Cardinal Wiseman

9 **What was the title of the Bishop of Woolwich's 1963 paperback which sold over a million copies?**

a. *God Today*
b. *Honest to God*
c. *God with us Now*
d. *The Joy of Being*

10 **How many of Jesus' disciples were fishermen?**

a. 2
b. 4
c. 1
d. 3

# CHASUBLES, COPES AND KEYS: CHRISTIAN SYMBOLS

1 Why was a fish often used by early Christians as a symbol of their faith?

2 What are the symbols of the four Evangelists?

3 Why are keys used as St Peter's symbols?

4 What colour were Easter eggs originally painted?

5 Why is the Holy Spirit symbolized by a dove?

6 How did the vestments of priests originate?

7 What is the botanical symbol of the Trinity?

8 Why are the weather vanes on church spires and towers depicted as cocks?

9 Why should a mythical creature, the unicorn, be used occasionally as a symbol associated with Mary, the mother of Jesus?

10 How many arms has the papal cross?

# CROSS SECTION

1 **According to Mark 1.6 John the Baptist ate locusts and what else in the wilderness?**
   a. Wild honey
   b. Pomegranates
   c. Figs
   d. Dates

2 **Who was Solomon's mother?**
   a. Abigail
   b. Ruth
   c. Naomi
   d. Bathsheba

3 **In which city was Johann Sebastian Bach employed from 1723 until his death, the period in which his chief religious works were composed?**
   a. Vienna
   b. Prague
   c. Leipzig
   d. Bonn

4 **In the second half of the fifteenth century which city was claimed by leaders of the Russian Church to be the 'Third Rome'?**
   a. Moscow
   b. St Petersburg
   c. Kiev
   d. Odessa

5 **In which year was the Roman Catholic movement Opus Dei founded?**
   a. 1896
   b. 1919
   c. 1938
   d. 1968

6 **Which is the shortest book of the Old Testament?**
   a. Hosea
   b. Amos
   c. Obadiah
   d. Jonah

7 **Which of these is the correct ending to this Beatitude from the Sermon on the Mount,'Blessed are the peace makers: . . .'?**

a. '. . . for they shall be called the children of God.'
b. '. . . for they shall see God.'
c. '. . . for they shall inherit the earth.'
d. '. . . for their's is the kingdom of heaven.'

8 **Where did Moses flee to after killing an Egyptian who was beating a Hebrew slave?**

a. Midian
b. Moab
c. Caria
d. Lydia

9 **Who survived when Jericho was destroyed?**

a. Rahab and her family
b. Deborah and her family
c. Sarah and her family
d. Martha and her family

10 **Who were the first Gentiles to believe in Christ?**

a. The Roman soldiers at his crucifixion
b. The Magi
c. St Paul's first converts in Rome
d. The Thessalonians

# MASSES, PASSIONS AND SPIRITUALS: CHRISTIAN MUSIC

1 Which Old Testament prophetess took a timbrel in her hand; and all the women went out after her with timbrels and with dances. And...answered them, 'Sing ye to the Lord, for he hath triumphed gloriously; the horse and his rider hath he thrown into the sea'?

2 In which oratorio do we find this prophetess's song?

3 Whose *Vespers* and *Mass* of the Virgin won him a position as composer at St Mark's, Venice?

4 In the nineteenth century there was an attempt to revive music in the Roman Catholic Church, looking back to a golden age of sixteenth-century compositions. It was called the Cecilian Movement; why?

5 Which composer died whilst working on a requiem commissioned from him by a mysterious visitor, whose visit filled him with foreboding that the requiem did indeed herald his own death?

6 During the Great Awakening in nineteenth-century America there were big outdoor gatherings referred to as Camp meetings attended by blacks and whites. What religious music grew out of this phenomenon?

7 Why were Gregorian chants so called?

8 Who was Homer Alvan Rodeheaver?

9 Which composer revived interest in Bach's great *St Matthew Passion* by a perfomance of it given in a Berlin concert hall in 1829?

10 What was the source material for Britten's composition *Noye's Fludde*?

# CROSS SECTION

1 **In December 1989 the Romanian dictatorship attempted to arrest the dissident priest Laszlo Tokes, sparking off the popular uprising that led to its downfall. Where did this take place?**
   a. Bucharest
   b. Cluj
   c. Braşov
   d. Timişoara

2 **Who is said to have laid the egg which Luther hatched?**
   a. St Paul
   b. Erasmus
   c. Calvin
   d. Wycliffe

3 **Which event led to the effective loss of Asia Minor for the Greek Orthodox Church?**
   a. The signing of the Versailles Treaty in 1919
   b. The fall of Constantinople in 1453
   c. The fall of Smyrna (Izmir) in 1922
   d. The Turkish invasion of Cyprus in 1974

4 **How many sacraments did Peter Lombard enumerate in his celebrated work referred to as the 'Sentences'?**
   a. 30
   b. 7
   c. 12
   d. 16

5 **What is the name of the door in the façade of St Peter's, Rome, nearest the Vatican Palace?**
   a. The Holy Door
   b. The Papal Door
   c. The Vatican Door
   d. The Mighty Door

6 **In which city did I. Hecker found the Missionary Society of St Paul the Apostle in 1858?**
   a. London
   b. Brussels
   c. New York
   d. Buenos Aires

7 **To which religious body did Joseph Meldicott Scriven, best known as the author of 'What a Friend We Have in Jesus', belong?**
   a. Baptists
   b. Mormons
   c. Plymouth Brethren
   d. Seventh-Day Adventists

8 **Which was the first metropolitan see in the United States, established by the Vatican in 1808?**
   a. Baltimore
   b. New Orleans
   c. Boston
   d. Philadelphia

9 **Who raised the spectre of Samuel, which revealed to Saul his imminent defeat by the Philistines and death?**
   a. Achish
   b. Asahel
   c. The Witch of En-Dor
   d. Eliphaz

10 **To whom did Baruch act as secretary?**
   a. Amos
   b. Malachi
   c. Paul
   d. Jeremiah

# LIFE OF CHRIST

1 How many days old was Mary's son when he was circumcised and called Jesus?

2 How many years pass in obscurity between Jesus' presentation at the Temple where he discourses knowledgeably with the teachers and his baptism by John?

3 Why did Zacchaeus climb a tree when Jesus visited Jericho?

4 Which two Old Testament characters appear with the radiant figure of Jesus during the transfiguration?

5 Where did Jesus' arrest take place?

6 Which miracle does John's Gospel describe as being the first sign of Jesus' special mission?

7 How were the disciples to find the upper room in which they were to prepare the Last Supper?

8 Who said at Jesus' death,'Truly this man was the Son of God'?

9 What is the first thing that Jesus does after his baptism by John?

10 Who is ordered to carry Jesus' cross for him to Golgotha?

# CROSS SECTION

1 **In which European country was the religious community of Taizé founded?**
  a. Switzerland
  b. Belgium
  c. Luxembourg
  d. France

2 **Wreaths made of different materials symbolize different attributes in Christian art. What does a wreath made of cypress signify?**
  a. Immortality
  b. Mourning
  c. Strength
  d. Victory over persecution

3 **When is Low Sunday?**
  a. First Sunday after Easter
  b. Sunday before Advent Sunday
  c. First Sunday after All Saints' Day
  d. First Sunday after Christmas

4 **Why was Samuel Crowther a significant figure in the history of the African Church?**
  a. He was the first black Anglican Bishop of Nigeria
  b. He was the first black Roman Catholic martyr
  c. He undertook the first translation of the Bible into an African language
  d. He was the founder of the first independent Church in Africa

5 **What was the English name given to the group of German Evangelical Christians which came together in 1934 in defiance of the Nazi-sponsored Church?**
  a. German Free Church
  b. Just Church
  c. Confessing Church
  d. Holy German Church

6 **Who was the first pope to set foot in Latin America?**
a. Paul VI
b. John Paul II
c. Paul IV
d. John XXIII

7 **In which cathedral did Benjamin Britten's *War Requiem* receive its first performance?**
a. Cologne
b. Canterbury
c. Carlisle
d. Coventry

8 **What does the word 'gospel', mean?**
a. Good news
b. God's story
c. God's writings
d. God's wisdom

9 **Who would normally wear a wimple?**
a. A bishop
b. A Greek Orthodox priest
c. A nun
d. An Anglican curate

10 **In 1984 the Vatican mediated a boundary dispute between which two South American countries?**
a. Venezuela and Brazil
b. Bolivia and Peru
c. Brazil and Paraguay
d. Chile and Argentina

# CHRISTIAN FESTIVALS

1 What day is All Saints' Day?

2 What day is All Souls' Day?

3 In France and New Orleans, Shrove Tuesday is celebrated as Mardi Gras. What does 'Mardi Gras' mean in English?

4 What is the date of Santa Nikolaus' (also known as Santa Claus) feast?

5 Why do priests and ministers, including the pope, wash the feet of members of their congregations on Maundy Thursday?

6 How do the inhabitants of Brockworth, Gloucestershire celebrate Whit Monday?

7 Some church feasts fall on different dates each year, for example Easter and Whitsun. Are there any feasts which always fall on the same day?

8 In the old days, 1 August or Lammas Day was celebrated in a special way. How?

9 How may the name of 'Easter' link the Church's festival to old pagan rites?

10 How is popcorn linked with Thanksgiving?

# CROSS SECTION

1 **Which Irish saint founded a convent at Kildare and in whose memory the nuns kept a fire burning?**
  a. St Patrick
  b. St Columba
  c. St Brigid
  d. St Brendan

2 **What happened to the Anglican Church in Ireland in 1871?**
  a. Five bishops left the Church
  b. It was disestablished
  c. Married men were admitted to the priesthood
  d. It produced its own prayer book

3 **Who is generally thought to be the 'beloved disciple'?**
  a. John
  b. James
  c. Peter
  d. Andrew

4 **When did the Russian Orthodox Church join the World Council of Churches?**
  a. 1950
  b. 1989
  c. 1961
  d. 1974

5 **Who had the original idea for the TV film *Jesus of Nazareth* starring Robert Powell?**
  a. John Kennedy
  b. Donald Coggan
  c. Pope Paul VI
  d. Harold Wilson

6 **Peter and which other disciple were miraculously freed from prison?**
  a. Timothy
  b. James
  c. Nathaniel
  d. Paul

7 **Which is the first of the Thirty-Nine Articles of Religion?**

a. Of Christ the Son of God
b. Of the Old Testament
c. Of Faith in the Holy Trinity
d. Of the Holy Ghost

8 **'It seemed good to me also, . . .to write unto thee . . . most excellent Theophilus.' Who writes thus at the start of his Gospel?**

a. Matthew
b. Mark
c. Luke
d. John

9 **Which Archbishop of Canterbury visited Pope Paul VI in Rome in 1966?**

a. Archbishop Coggan
b. Archbishop Temple
c. Archbishop Ramsey
d. Archbishop Fisher

10 **The members of which Protestant denomination are also referred to as Campbellites because of the influence of two of its founder members?**

a. Disciples of Christ
b. Christian Reformed Church in North America
c. Christian Methodist Episcopal Church
d. Church of the Nazarene

# THE ANGELIC HOST

1 To whom was an angel talking when he said 'Lift up your eyes and see, all the goats that leap upon the flock were striped, spotted and mottled'?

2 Who does Paul say shall judge the angels?

3 Who tells Zechariah that his wife Elizabeth will bear a son called John?

4 With what heavenly creatures does Solomon embellish the inner sanctuary of his Temple to the Lord?

5 Why in Christian tradition is Michael the archangel often depicted fighting a dragon?

6 How many choirs of angels were there thought to be?

7 What were the Angels of Mons?

8 Which angel is referred to by Milton in *Paradise Lost* as the 'sociable spirit'?

9 In the Book of Tobit, Tobias goes to Ecbatana where he will meet his future wife Sarah in the company of two other beings. Who or what are they?

10 When Peter is released by an angel from his imprisonment by Herod what does he first think is happening to him?

# CROSS SECTION

1 **The Greek word 'paraclete' is used in John's Gospel to refer to what?**
a. A government official
b. A church festival
c. A kind of church
d. The Holy Spirit

2 **Which name did Cardinal Roncalli taken when he was elected to the papacy?**
a. John XXIII
b. John Paul I
c. Paul VI
d. Paul III

3 **In what year did Thomas Bray and colleagues found SPCK?**
a. 1925
b. 1698
c. 1789
d. 1856

4 **In which African country did the prophetess Alice Lenshina evangelize during the 1950s and 1960s?**
a. South Africa
b. Ghana
c. Togo
d. Zambia

5 **Which eighteenth-century English Methodist evangelist split from Wesley to form a Calvinistic movement, preached to huge outdoor congregations in England and America, dying near Boston in 1769?**
a. John Fletcher
b. Francis Asbury
c. Thomas Coke
d. George Whitefield

6 **Where was Zacharias when he saw the angel Gabriel who told him that Elizabeth, his wife, would give birth to a son, though both of them were getting on in years?**
   a. In the Temple
   b. In his fields
   c. In his bed
   d. On the road to Jerusalem

7 **In which Latin American country is the Virgin of Guadalupe a focal point of national devotion?**
   a. Mexico
   b. Bolivia
   c. Ecuador
   d. Peru

8 **Who preached a famous sermon in 1843 entitled 'The Parting of Friends'?**
   a. John Henry Newman
   b. Charles Darwin
   c. Benjamin Disraeli
   d. John Keble

9 **Which of the books in the Bible was inspired by visions experienced by the writer while exiled on the island of Patmos?**
   a. The Acts
   b. Epistle of James
   c. Jonah
   d. Revelation

10 **How did Samson wreak vengeance on the Philistines once his strength had returned?**
   a. He demolished the temple to their god Dagon killing himself and all inside
   b. He led a victorious force against them
   c. He poisoned the flour from which their bread was baked
   d. He destroyed their supplies of winter corn

# CHURCH ORNAMENTS, SACRED OBJECTS AND TREASURES

1 What is the name of the cup or goblet used to contain the wine for Communion?

2 What is a thurible used for?

3 To which of Henry VIII's wives did a beautiful cup belong, now one of the treasured possessions of St John the Baptist's Church, Cirencester, Gloucestershire?

4 Where can one see a remarkable medieval map of the world, the Mappa Mundi, the proposed sale of which caused a national uproar?

5 In St Peter's Church, Marlow, Buckinghamshire there is a mummified hand, said to be a relic of which saint?

6 What is a ciborium?

7 Which artist do we associate primarily with the frescos depicting the life of St Francis at Assisi?

8 Which two sacred sites in Jerusalem did the Emperor Constantine enclose with a church in the fourth century?

9 What is the name of the staff, shaped like an ornate shepherd's crook, carried by bishops?

10 What Parisian church was built by St Louis IX in the thirteenth century to house his collection of sacred relics, including, it is said, the Crown of Thorns?

# CROSS SECTION

1 **Charles de Foucauld, the former French cavalry officer and Trappist monk, who was murdered in 1916, became known as the Hermit of where?**
   a. Hermit of the Alps
   b. Hermit of Corsica
   c. Hermit of the Levant
   d. Hermit of the Sahara

2 **In Jesus' parable of the sower, what happened to the seeds that fell by the way side?**
   a. They were choked by weeds
   b. They were scorched by the sun
   c. They were eaten by birds
   d. They became diseased and died

3 **What was the title of Evelyn Underhill's work, published in 1911, which came to be regarded as a definitive treatment of its subject?**
   a. *Faith in the Trinity*
   b. *Handmaiden of the Lord*
   c. *Mysticism*
   d. *Miracles*

4 **What is the meaning of the phrase *auto de fe* which formed an integral public ceremony in the Spanish Inquisition?**
   a. Act of faith
   b. Change of religion
   c. Self-punishment
   d. Trial by iron

5 **Who annexed the Papal States, forcing Pope Pius VII into five years' exile?**
   a. Garibaldi
   b. Wellington
   c. Napoleon
   d. Mussolini

**6 Which parliamentary Act confirmed Henry VIII and his successors 'the only supreme head on earth of the Church of England'?**

a. Act of Division
b. Act of Supremacy
c. Act of National Faith
d. Act of Secession

**7 How many churches have been built above the traditional tomb of Peter in Rome?**

a. 4
b. 1
c. 2
d. 7

**8 After whom does Gregorian chant take its name?**

a. Pope Gregory I
b. Gregory of Nyssa
c. Gregory of Athens
d. Gregory of Tyre

**9 Where was Robert Schuller's church the Crystal Cathedral constructed?**

a. Miami, Florida
b. Calgary, Alberta
c. Orange County, California
d. Juneau, Alaska

**10 According to Exodus, how did Aaron use his rod to defeat the Pharaoh's magicians?**

a. He paralysed them
b. He beat them with it
c. It turned into a serpent which bit them
d. It turned into a serpent and devoured the serpents created by the magicians from their rods

# THE DEVIL AND ALL HIS WORKS

1 What did the word 'Satan' mean in Hebrew?

2 In the Book of Revelation, St John tells how an angel bound Satan and threw him into a bottomless pit. How long must he remain bound and captive until 'he must be loosed a little season'?

3 In which of Dostoevsky's novels do two brothers argue about the problem of the existence of so much evil in the world and its implications concerning the existence of a loving merciful God?

4 Why was Jesus' resurrection a triumph, too, over the devil?

5 What is the name of C. S. Lewis' work which purports to be a collection of letters from an older devil to his nephew?

6 To whom is Jesus talking when he says 'I beheld Satan as lightning fall from heaven. Behold, I give unto you power to tread on serpents and scorpions, and over all the power of the enemy'?

7 Which priests are allowed to perform the exorcism rite contained in the Rituale Romanum?

8 Who wrote a series of novels concerning satanism of a particularly lurid nature, including *The Devil Rides Out*?

9 What is one of the devil's names which means 'Lord of the Flies'?

10 Which ancient city is used by John in the Book of Revelation to represent evil and wickedness?

# CROSS SECTION

1 **Popularly known as the White Fathers, this brotherhood was founded in 1868 as the Society of Missionaries of . . . where?**
   a. Africa
   b. The Andes
   c. The Great Plains
   d. Siberia

2 **According to tradition how many weeks in Lent form Passiontide?**
   a. 1 week
   b. 2 weeks
   c. 4 weeks
   d. 6 weeks

3 **What was the Sanhedrin?**
   a. The altar in Solomon's Temple
   b. Another name for the cities of refuge
   c. King David's élite bodyguard
   d. The Jewish high court

4 **Who established a reformed Church in Scotland in 1560?**
   a. Mary Queen of Scots
   b. Lord Murray
   c. John Knox
   d. James III

5 **What was the name given to the often beautifully illustrated prayer books used by noble and wealthy laity in the Middle Ages?**
   a. Books of Hours
   b. Books of Discipline
   c. Books of Devotion
   d. Books of Office

6 **Which of the Apostles was a man of Kerioth?**
   a. Simon
   b. Judas
   c. John
   d. Andrew

7 **Why did the theologian Karl Barth leave his academic life in Germany to take up a professorial position in Switzerland?**

a. Because he disagreed with the German academic establishment
b. Because he was born in Switzerland
c. Because of his opposition to Hitler and the Nazis
d. Because of his disagreement with Lutheran doctrine

8 **Which English sovereign put an end to the payment of Peter's Pence?**

a. Henry I
b. Richard I
c. Henry VIII
d. James II

9 **Why was the wandering Jew condemned to wander this earth until Christ's Second Coming?**

a. He struck Jesus and told him to hurry to his death
b. As a symbol of the dispersal of the Jews
c. He was one of the moneylenders in the Temple
d. He refused Christ a drink on his way to Calvary

10 **Which nineteenth-century French artist provided illustrations for the works of Dante, Milton and the Bible?**

a. Monet
b. Renoir
c. Ingres
d. Doré

# FOOD AND DRINK

1 Why was the Bishop's Bible of 1568 called also the 'Treacle Bible'?

2 What biblical food was 'like coriander seed, white, and the taste of it was like wafers made with honey'?

3 This was the menu for what famous meal: venison stew, stuffed wild turkey, oysters, sweet corn and, for desert, pumpkin with maple syrup?

4 For what did Esau sell his birthright to Jacob?

5 What was the first temptation experienced by Jesus in the wilderness?

6 Why was an eighteenth-century version of the Bible called the 'Vinegar Bible'?

7 At the Last Supper, Jesus gave his disciples bread and wine but, being the Passover, what meat might they have eaten?

8 How was the wine produced by Jesus' miracle at the marriage in Cana different to the wine originally served before it ran out?

9 After seven years of famine in Canaan and Egypt, Jacob sends his sons to Joseph in Egypt to buy what commodity?

10 When Jesus is returning to Jerusalem from Bethany he curses a tree. Why?

# CROSS SECTION

1 **In 1842 George Augustus Selwyn was apppointed the first Anglican bishop of where?**
   a. New Zealand
   b. South Africa
   c. Canada
   d. Australia

2 **What religious significance do escallop shells reveal on a coat of arms?**
   a. Ordination
   b. Pilgrimage
   c. Conversion
   d. Martyrdom

3 **Where did Jesus walk on the water?**
   a. On the Sea of Galilee
   b. On the River Jordan
   c. On the Dead Sea
   d. On the Mediterranean Sea

4 **In which Asian capital did the World Council of Churches organize a convocation on Justice, Peace and the Integrity of Creation in 1990?**
   a. Bangkok
   b. Singapore
   c. Seoul
   d. Tokyo

5 **Who, in the New Testament, was Malchus?**
   a. A Roman centurion
   b. A servant of the high priest whose right ear was cut off when Jesus was arrested
   c. One of the criminals crucified with Jesus
   d. One of the Magi

6 **When did the Book of Common Prayer cease to carry services to commemorate the Gunpowder Plot, the execution of Charles I and the restoration of Charles II?**

a. 1701
b. 1789
c. 1832
d. 1859

7 **Where was the first Christian Church in Europe established?**

a. Philippi
b. Rome
c. Milan
d. Naples

8 **Which major event led to the closing of all Christian churches in China?**

a. Death of Mao
b. Start of the Cultural Revolution
c. Trial of the Gang of Four
d. The Vietnam War

9 **Which land did God promise to the Israelites?**

a. Goshen
b. Canaan
c. Gilead
d. Ammon

10 **Who, in the Middles Ages, was known as Longinus?**

a. Pilate's deputy
b. The soldier who thrust his spear into Jesus' side?
c. The master of the ship in which Paul was wrecked
d. The bridegroom at the wedding at Cana

# TURNS OF PHRASE

1 Who tells us not to cast pearls before swine?

2 At the Day of Judgement the Son of Man will separate 'the sheep from the goats'. Which will go on his left side and which on his right?

3 Who in the Old Testament first felt he had escaped by the skin of his teeth?

4 What in Proverbs is 'the principal thing; therefore get . . . and with all thy getting get understanding'?

5 Where does the phrase 'in the twinkling of an eye' come from?'

6 Who lays down these laws to the Israelites: 'And if any mischief follow, then thou shalt give life for life, Eye for eye, tooth for tooth, hand for hand, foot for foot'?

7 What happens, according to Jesus, 'if the blind lead the blind'?

8 In which parable does Christ use these words, 'For many are called, but few are chosen'?

9 Which eighteenth to nineteenth-century English visionary and poet wrote these lines in his Everlasting Gospel?

*Both read the Bible day and night,*
*But thou read'st black where I read white*

10 In the New Testament what shall 'cover a multitude of sins'?

# CROSS SECTION

1 **Before his conversion to more orthodox Christianity, Augustine of Hippo belonged to which heretical sect?**
   a. Donatises
   b. Gnostics
   c. Manichees
   d. Ebimites

2 **When was the Society for the Propagation of the Gospel in Foreign Parts founded in London?**
   a. 1701
   b. 1861
   c. 1801
   d. 1751

3 **Which New England settlement was the site of the first Congregational church in the USA and of the witchcraft trials of 1692?**
   a. Plymouth, Massachusetts
   b. Salem, Massachusetts
   c. Rhode Island
   d. Germantown, Pennsylvania

4 **What is Thomism?**
   a. The theology of Thomas Aquinas
   b. The theology of Thomas à Kempis
   c. The beliefs of the Thomas Christians of India
   d. The teachings of the apochryphal Gospel of Thomas

5 **Who said, 'We shall not rest until we have rooted out Christianity'?**
   a. Diocletian
   b. Himmler
   c. Herod Antipas
   d. Mao Tse-tung

6 **What number psalm is 'The Lord is my shepherd'?**
   a. Psalm 16
   b. Psalm 19
   c. Psalm 23
   d. Psalm 46

7 **What caused the previously close Barnabas and Paul to work apart?**

a. They could not agree which country to visit next
b. They disagreed about taking John Mark with them on a second journey
c. They couldn't get on well together
d. They decided they would spread the gospel more quickly independently

8 **Which future king of England was forced to renounce his post as Lord High Admiral because of his Roman Catholic faith?**

a. Charles II
b. James II
c. William IV
d. King John

9 **In which Latin American country was a Church of the People encouraged by the government which came to power in 1979?**

a. El Salvador
b. Nicaragua
c. Guatemala
d. Costa Rica

10 **Where did St Jerome, who translated most of the Bible into Latin, settle in 386 to rule the men's monastery and devote his life to study?**

a. Avignon
b. Constantinople
c. Bethlehem
d. Alexandria

# THE SECOND COMING

1 To what, in the New Testament and since, does the Greek word *parousia* generally refer?

2 What is the name usually given to the 1000 years when Christ, having returned to earth, will reign with the saints before returning with them to heaven?

3 An American Baptist minister, William Miller, calculated from studies of the Bible that the Second Coming would take place in 1843 or 1844. Although both dates passed, his followers organized themselves into which religious movement?

4 Whose New Testament description of the period just before the Second Coming is this: 'Immediately after the tribulation of those days shall the sun be darkened, and the moon shall not give her light, and the stars shall fall from heaven'?

5 In which Epistle is Christ's coming described thus, 'The day of the Lord will come as a thief in the night'?

6 In medieval churches the Last Judgement was often carved and sculpted in the tympanum. Where on the church was this?

7 What is the name given in John's Epistles for one of the decievers who appear because 'it is the last time'?

8 Which Apostle speaks of 'a man of sin' and a 'son of perdition' who sets himself up as an evil opponent of God, but who will be destroyed when Christ returns?

9 Which sect, originating in America, believe that 144,000 of their number will rule with Christ over the earth in the Theocratic Kingdom?

10 What is the name given in the Book of Revelation for the place where a final battle takes place between the powers of this earth and heaven?

# CROSS SECTION

1 **John Paul II is the first non-Italian pope since which year?**
   a. 1523
   b. 1623
   c. 1723
   d. 1823

2 **How did the twentieth-century American Trappist monk and writer, Thomas Merton, die?**
   a. Through an extended fast
   b. By catching cold brought on by austere practices
   c. Electrocuted by a faulty electric fan
   d. Murdered by a repressive South American régime

3 **Corrie Ten Boom, the devout Christian and member of the Dutch resistance movement, lived and worked in her father's shop in Haarlem which became a refuge for Jews during the Nazi Occupation. What kind of shop was it?**
   a. Watchmaker
   b. Barber
   c. Florist
   d. Jeweller

4 **In which city did the charismatic missionary Jackie Pullinger work amongst the destitute?**
   a. Saigon
   b. Beijing
   c. Bangkok
   d. Hong Kong

5 **What is the name of the magazine of the Iona Community?**
   a. *Coracle*
   b. *The Columban*
   c. *The Islander*
   d. *The Celtic Mission*

6 **Which Hollywood actor stars as Indiana Jones in the adventure film *Raiders of the Lost Ark*, concerning a thrilling search for the lost Ark of the Covenant?**
   a. Christopher Reeve
   b. Robert Redford
   c. Harrison Ford
   d. Donald Sutherland

7 **Why is the last Sunday after Trinity called Stir Up Sunday?**
   a. Oliver Cromwell gave an oration on that day which stirred people up to join the Parliamentary cause
   b. 'Stir up' are the first two words of the collect for that day
   c. Traditionally, the congregation was exhorted to stir themselves and be ready for Lent
   d. It was a Sunday when quarrelling married couples were urged to come to terms and be at peace

8 **What were the catacombs?**
   a. Early underground Christian burial places
   b. Secret early churches
   c. Writings from the Cathar sect
   d. An instrument of torture used by the Romans

9 **Who wrote the influential devotional work *Introduction to the Devout Life* in 1608?**
   a. Francis Xavier
   b. Francis of Sales
   c. Ignatius Loyola
   d. Teresa of Avila

10 **Who was Cotton Mather?**
   a. An escpaed slave turned evangelist
   b. A Christian plantation owner
   c. One of the Pilgrim fathers of the *Mayflower*
   d. A Boston minister, author of *Magnalia Christi Americana*

# HEAVEN AND HELL: THE AFTERLIFE

1 In the parable of the rich man and Lazarus, when both have died and the rich man languishes in hell, with whom does he see Lazarus?

2 From which book of the New Testament does the image of heaven's 'pearly gates' derive?

3 Who tells us 'We shall not all sleep, but we shall be changed . . .' before uttering the saying, 'O death, where is thy sting? O grave, where is thy victory'?

4 What was the Hebrew name used in the Old Testament for the underworld of the dead?

5 From which of Shakespeare's plays comes these lines?.

*Angels and ministers of grace defend us!*
*Be thou a spirit of health or goblin damn'd,*
*Bring with thee airs from heaven or blasts from hell.*

6 To whom does Jesus say,'Today thou shalt be with me in paradise'?

7 What in Christian tradition are the 'four last things'?

8 In Roman Catholic doctrine there is, after death, a stage before heaven when souls are cleansed of sin. What is this stage called?

9 Which Italian poet wrote the *Divine Comedy*, in which he visualizes a journey through hell, purgatory and paradise?

10 In the 'comfortable words' in the Book of Common Prayer we hear the words 'So God loved the world, that he gave his only begotten Son, to the end that all that believe in him should not perish, but have everlasting life'. What is the origin of these words?

# CROSS SECTION

1 **Where did the League of Militant Godless have its origin in 1925?**
   a. Bolshevik Russia
   b. Fascist Italy
   c. The Weimar Republic of Germany
   d. China

2 **Roughly what percentage of the world's population adhere to Christianity?**
   a. 20 per cent
   b. 15 per cent
   c. 33 per cent
   d. 55 per cent

3 **What brought about the Catholic Reformation, as it is sometimes known, in the sixteenth century?**
   a. The Great Schism
   b. The Babylonian Captivity
   c. The rise of Protestantism
   d. The fall of Constantinople

4 **How did the Coptic Church get its name?**
   a. Because of its liturgical language
   b. Because it was founded by St Copatia
   c. Because its priests are called Copti
   d. Because it was first established in the ancient Middle Eastern kingdom of Coptia

5 **The name Jesus is derived from a Hebrew word with a root meaning what?**
   a. To conquer
   b. To save
   c. To teach
   d. To share

6 **Which doctrine was adopted by the Roman Catholic Church on 18 July 1870?**
a. Immaculate Conception
b. Divine Right of Kings
c. Celibacy for ordained clergy
d. Papal Infallibility

7 **Where in the Anglican community was the term Protestant first officially used in the name of the Church?**
a. North America
b. Wales
c. Africa
d. England

8 **Which saint's day is celebrated on the last day of November?**
a. St Luke
b. St Andrew
c. St Mark
d. St Peter

9 **Who, according to the Book of Mormon, led a group of Hebrews to America in 600 BC?**
a. Mormon
c. The prophet Lehi
d. Moroni
e. Urim

10 **Originally called Thomasites after their founder, what are members of this Christian sect now called?**
a. Disciples of Christ
b. Reformed Baptists
c. Christadelphians
d. Evangelical Lutherans

# A CHRISTIAN BESTIARY

1 What special mark is said to be seen on an ass's back as a commemoration of the fact that an ass bore Christ into Jerusalem on Palm Sunday?

2 What was special about the stag St Eustace saw whilst out hunting one day, a sight that brought about his conversion?

3 What Animal did Samson kill with his bare hands when he was a young man?

4 When Elisha is mocked by children for having a bald head, what animals appear and attack his tormentors?

5 What animal does God provide as a sacrifice in place of Abraham's son, Isaac?

6. Complete this phrase,'Ye blind guides, which strain at a gnat, and swallow a . . . '?

7 In one of Raphael's paintings the infant John the Baptist hands a small bird to the Christ-Child as a symbol of his Passion. What is the bird?

8 In the Song of Solomon which animals spoil the vines?

9 Two water creatures may have given rise to the 'Leviathan' of the Bible. Which were they?

10 The twelfth-century saint Hugh of Lincoln is usually represented by a swan. What is the reason for this?

# CROSS SECTION

1 **Where is the highest spire in Great Britain?**
   a. Salisbury
   b. Lincoln
   c. Exeter
   d. Lichfield

2 **In which country was the priest Camilo Torres active in the armed struggle against repression?**
   a. Argentina
   b. Ecuador
   c. Brazil
   d. Colombia

3 **Which is the only one of the disciples to have a wife mentioned in the Bible?**
   a. Judas
   b. Peter
   c. Matthew
   d. Thomas

4 **Why is Esther regarded as a Jewish heroine?**
   a. She persuaded her husband, the king of Persia, not to massacre the Jews in his realm
   b. She smuggled in food during a siege
   c. She killed Nebuchadnezzar's General Holofernes
   d. She led the Jews, dancing and singing, against the Philistine hordes

5 **Into how many houses is the General Synod of the Church of England divided?**
   a. 4
   b. 6
   c. 3
   d. 8

6 **Who said,'If God did not exist, it would be necessary to invent him'?**
   a. Oliver Cromwell
   b. Voltaire
   c. Benjamin Disraeli
   d. Oscar Wilde

7 **Who composed a 'Christmas Oratorio', nearly 300 church cantatas and a celebrated Mass in B Minor?**

a. W. F. Bach
b. C. P. E. Bach
c. J. S. Bach
d. J. C. Bach

8 **Which bishop of the United Methodist Church served as prime minister of Zimbabwe-Rhodesia in 1979?**

a. Robert Mugabe
b. Hastings Banda
c. Abel Muzorewa
d. Joshua Nkomo

9 **Who was the sister of Mary and Lazarus?**

a. Rebecca
b. Martha
c. Ruth
d. Sarah

10 **Where in the modern world is Mount Ararat, where Noah's ark came to rest?**

a. Iran
b. North Africa
c. Armenia
d. Saudi Arabia

# CONVERTS

1 Which Chinese statesman and nationalist General converted from Buddhism to Methodism?

2 Which English courtier and poet, renowned for his courtly accomplishments, wit and debauchery, was persuaded by Bishop Burnet to repent and convert back to his faith on his deathbed?

3 Who, after a lifetime in journalism and broadcasting, and as a vociferous critic of religion (in 1936 he published *The Earnest Atheist*), became a Roman Catholic in 1982?

4 Of whom did Jesus say, 'I say unto you, I have not found so great faith, no, not in Israel'?

5 Whose mission was to convert the English to Christianity, a task which he began by converting King Aethelbert of Kent and his subjects?

6 Which English-born American pastor set about converting Massachusetts Indians and translated the Bible into their language?

7 Which eighth-century saint was called the Apostle of Germany and was killed by pagans whilst conducting a confirmation service for converts?

8 When and where did the pop star Cliff Richard undergo his conversion?

9 A Carmelite nun and philosopher, Teresa Benedicta of the Cross, met her death in the gas chamber at Auschwitz in 1942. What was her religion before converting to Catholicism in 1922?

10 Which British athlete, a silver medallist in the 1984 Los Angeles Olympics, experienced baptism by the Holy Spirit in 1987 in a dream which effected his conversion?

# CROSS SECTION

1 **From whose boat did the Apostles cast the net which brought in the miraculous draft of fishes?**
   a. Simon's
   b. Timothy's
   c. Joseph's
   d. Matthew's

2 **In Proverbs what does pride go before?**
   a. A fall
   b. Despair
   c. Destruction
   d. A defeat

3 **What was Adam's ale?**
   a. Cider
   b. Water
   c. Beer
   d. Wine

4 **The first assembly of the the AACC took place in 1963. What do the initials AACC stand for?**
   a. All African Conference of Churches
   b. Anglo-African Church Council
   c. Afro-Asian Christian Community
   d. Allied Anglo-Catholic Conference

5 **When Elijah sought refuge in a mountain cave there came a great wind, an earthquake and a fire. What happened after the fire?**
   a. The rains fell
   b. Lightning struck the mountain top
   c. He saw an angelic host
   d. He heard a still small voice

6 **In which country was the first printed Bible produced?**
   a. Germany
   b. Italy
   c. England
   d. France

7 **With whom did Paul and Silas stay when they were in Thessalonica?**
a. Tobias
b. Michael
c. Philip
d. Jason

8 **What is meant by Transubstantiation?**
a. Resurrection
b. Levitation
c. Alchemy, which drew the disapproval of the Church
d. The changing of the substance of bread and wine into the body and blood of Christ during the Eucharist

9 **Who composed the oratorio *Belshazzar's Feast*?**
a. Benjamin Britten
b. Aaron Copland
c. William Walton
d. Francois Poulenc

10 **What did Salome take to the tomb on the morning of the resurrection?**
a. Spices to embalm the body
b. A shroud
c. Water
d. Flowers

# MONASTIC ORDERS

1 What name was given to the second order of the Franciscans?

2 To which Israelite sect is the community of Qumran, which bore many of the hallmarks of later monasticism, thought to have belonged?

3 Which fourteenth-century saint is regarded as the Father of Eastern Monasticism and established the practice of entering monastic life as an irrevocable act?

4 The members of which order were referred to as the 'white monks'?

5 Armand Jean Le Bouthillier de Rance, Abbot of La Trappe in Normandy, reformed his Cistercian monastery along very strict lines giving rise to which monastic communities?

6 The members of which order were referred to as Grey Friars when they first came to England?

7 Where does the word 'friar' come from?

8 Why were Capuchin friars so called?

9 Who were referred to as the Black Friars?

10 What is the name of the novelist Ellis Peter's Welsh detective monk?

# CROSS SECTION

1 **When the Lord decides to destroy Sodom and Gomorrah he strikes a bargain with Abraham to the effect that he will spare the cities if he finds a certain number of righteous men living in them. What number do they finally agree on?**
a. 10
b. 20
c. 1
d. 50

2 **Which of these is the odd one out?**
a. Ox
b. Ass
c. Lamb
d. Horse

3 **Which insect is mentioned most often in the Bible?**
a. Gnat
b. Locust
c. Fly
d. Ant

4 **In which town did Paul find an altar with the inscription 'To an unknown god'?**
a. Corinth
b. Ephesus
c. Athens
d. Rome

5 **Of all the books in the Bible, which is the most widely translated?**
a. Genesis
b. Gospel of Matthew
c. Gospel of Mark
d. Revelation

6 **From what was the *shofar* made which announced the start of religious festivals in Israel?**
a. A hollow branch fitted with a reed
b. An animal's horn
c. A goat skin stretched over an iron drum
d. Pipes made from papyrus reeds

7 **Whose brother 'is a hairy man'?**
a. Esau's
b. Isaac's
c. Jacob's
d. Joseph's

8 **Where was Jesus baptized?**
a. In Nazareth
b. In the River Jordan
c. In the Sea of Galilee
d. In the Temple

9 **In which country was Helder Camara archbishop in the 1960s and 1970s?**
a. Spain
b. Brazil
c. South Africa
d. Philippines

10 **Which saint bears the symbol of a gridiron, on which he was martyred?**
a. St Patrick
b. St Laurence
c. St Hugh
d. St George

# THE HEALING MINISTRY

1 Which of the four Gospel writers is believed to have been a doctor?

2 In John's Gospel, what does Jesus do when curing the blind man on the sabbath?

3 Which nineteenth-century missionary went out to Africa to use his medical training to alleviate suffering among the native population, but who became almost better known for his work as an explorer?

4 How did Jesus know, in spite of the crowds pressing round him, that the woman suffering from a haemorrhage had touched his robe and been cured?

5 What was the immediate effect on people wishing to be healed by Baptist minister and faith healer Kathryn Kuhlman when she placed her hands on their heads; a reaction she attributed to the 'power of the Holy Spirit'?

6 By what physical process do the sick pilgrims to Lourdes hope to be cured?

7 Mother Teresa of Calcutta founded an order which devotes itself to the care of the destitute and dying in India. What is the name of the order?

8 Why is it now thought references to lepers and leprosy in the Bible are misleading?

9 In 1862 a Boston woman believed she had been healed by one Phineas Quinty and went on to establish a Church that laid great emphasis on healing through the power of the mind and faith. The Church was the First Church of Christ, Scientist, what was the name of its founder?

10 How many cases of Christ raising people from the dead do we read of in the Gospels?

# CROSS SECTION

1 **Who was the author of the 1977 study of Black Theology, *Farewell to Innocence?***

a. Desmond Tutu
b. Frank Chicane
c. Alan Paton
d. Allan Boesak

2 **Where did the Tractarian Revival of the nineteenth century have its roots?**

a. Geneva
b. Florence
c. Oxford
d. New York

3 **To whom is Paul writing when he refers to old taboos such as 'touch not; taste not; handle not'?**

a. Corinthians
b. Colossians
c. Hebrews
d. Galatians

4 **In which scientific field did Teilhard de Chardin work, the results of which helped to inform his theological ideas?**

a. Physics
b. Astronomy
c. Palaeontology
d. Chemistry

5 **Which town was David's capital before he captured Jerusalem?**

a. Bethlehem
b. Hebron
c. Nazareth
d. Kerioth

6 **What was the name given to the religious movement founded by Frank Buchman in 1938?**
   a. Moral Rearmament
   b. Forward in Faith
   c. Conquering Crusaders
   d. Moravian Brethren

7 **Into which land did Joseph and Mary flee with Jesus to escape Herod's persecution?**
   a. Canaan
   b. Samaria
   c. Syria
   d. Egypt

8 **Who was the author of *Absalom, Absalom!* and *Go Down Moses*?**
   a. Nathaniel Hawthorne
   b. Walker Percy
   c. William Faulkner
   d. Mark Twain

9 **The Japanese evangelist Toyohiko Kagawa began his pastoral work in the slums of which Japanese city?**
   a. Kobe
   b. Tokyo
   c. Sapporo
   d. Osaka

10 **There were six cities of refuge. Who could find asylum in them?**
   a. Those who had accidentally caused the death of another
   b. Gentiles living in Palestine amongst the Jewish tribes
   c. Enemies who had surrendered
   d. Debtors

# THE POPES

1 Who is regarded by the Roman Catholic Church as having been the first pope?

2 Which treaty signed on 11 February 1929 'finally and irrevocably' established the Vatican City as a sovereign state?

3 Which twentieth-century pope's sudden death during the night gave rise to wild rumours of assassination?

4 What is the name given to the female pope who, for centuries, was believed to have existed?

5 Which pope, after the sentence had been deferred for a number of years, finally excommunicated Henry VIII of England?

6 During which century was the papacy moved from Rome to Avignon?

7 Which twentieth-century pope gained a reputation for his liberal approach and convoked the council known as Vatican II?

8 What were anti-popes?

9 How did Pope Leo I, or 'the Great', save Rome from destruction in 452?

10 Why is the pope's residence in Rome called the Vatican?

# CROSS SECTION

1 **Who said,'I have fought a good fight, I have finished my course, I have kept the faith'?**
a. Paul
b. Stephen
c. Jesus
d. Peter

2 **When Herod commanded the Massacre of the Holy Innocents, who were his intended victims?**
a. Male children under two years old
b. All children under the age of three
c. Male children under the age of four
d. Male children less than a year old

3 **Which birds are said to have fed Elijah when he was in hiding?**
a. Gulls
b. Ravens
c. Crows
d. Hawks

4 **How did the Jews avoid being destroyed when God 'smote all the first-born in the land of Egypt'?**
a. They left the country
b. They covered their heads
c. They marked their doorways with the blood of the Passover lamb
d. They prayed all night

5 **In which South American country did the Jesuits organize self-contained villages for the native Indians run on ecclesiastical lines from 1650 to 1720?**
a. Venezuela
b. Chile
c. Paraguay
d. Bolivia

6 **Which biblical city was excavated between 1922 and 1934 by the archeological team directed by Sir Leonard Woolley?**

a. Jericho
b. Ephesus
c. Ur
d. Alexandria

7 **Who was killed at Achor (Trouble Valley) because he disobeyed a command from God?**

a. Achan
b. Potiphar
c. Jethro
d. Achish

8 **Who is the patron saint of actors?**

a. St Vitus
b. St Cuthbert
c. St Pancras
d. St Ivo

9 **What made Peter realize that Jesus' prophecy of his denial had come true?**

a. Jesus looked at him
b. One of the people in the courtyard reminded him of it
c. Another disciple pointed it out
d. Hearing the cock crow

10 **For how many years were the Jews slaves in Egypt?**

a. 220
b. 111
c. 300
d. 430

# CHRISTIAN LITERATURE

1 Which book in the Old Testament is renowned for its poetic beauty and lyrical description of the joys of love between man and woman?

2 Whose diaries, discovered and published in the 1930s, give a vivid description of his life as a clergyman on the borders of Wales and England?

3 Which English poet, having written passionate and witty love poems, published as *Songs and Sonnets*, later wrote the celebrated *Divine Poems* and became Dean of St Paul's in 1621?

4 Which American poet became a recluse at the age of twenty-three and produced well over a thousand remarkable poems, many with a spiritual content, including 'My life closed twice before its close' and 'Because I could not stop for Death'?

5 Who wrote *The Vision of William Concerning Piers the Plowman*?

6 Which American author's book *Death Comes for the Archbishop* deals with the life and work of a Catholic archbishop and his flock in the south-west of the USA?

7 In 1743 Handel wrote his oratorio *Samson*, using which earlier English literary work as his libretto?

8 The best-selling author Lloyd C. Douglas wrote a novel concerning a young Roman tribune present at the crucifixion and the effect this has on his subsequent life. What is its title?

9 The famous Christian work *The Dark Night of the Soul* was written by which Spanish mystic?

10 The dean of St Patrick's Cathedral, Dublin, who wrote *Gulliver's Travels*, had earlier published *A Tale of a Tub*, a satire on religious dissension. What was his name?

# CROSS SECTION

1 **What did Jesus use, according to St John's Gospel, to help him drive the money changers and others from the Temple?**
   a. A small whip
   b. A stick
   c. A stool
   d. A broom

2 **What use did both Jews and Romans put to nails from crucifixion crosses?**
   a. A means of healing
   b. A temple offering
   c. A way of warding off evil spirits
   d. Good luck charms

3 **Where was Jesus when he said,'A prophet is not without honour, save in his own country, and in his own house'?**
   a. Galilee
   b. Jerusalem
   c. Samaria
   d. In the wilderness

4 **With which period in Christian history is baroque art most closely associated?**
   a. Reformation
   b. Counter-Reformation
   c. Great Schism
   d. Nineteenth-century evangelical expansion

5 **At what stage in Christian history were the four Gospels first described as such?**
   a. In the first century
   b. In the second century
   c. In the tenth century
   d. In the eleventh century

6 **To whom was Paul writing when he proffered the advice, 'Drink no longer water, but use a little wine for thy stomach's sake and thine often infirmities'?**

a. Barnabas
b. Luke
c. Timothy
d. John Mark

7 **In 1983 Josef Glemp was named Archbishop of where?**

a. Budapest
b. Prague
c. Warsaw
d. Bucharest

8 **Which Carmelite nun is portrayed in Christian art carrying a bunch of roses and became known as 'The Little Flower'.**

a. St Bernadette of Lourdes
b. St Teresa of Avila
c. St Clare of Assisi
d. St Theresa of Lisieux

9 **Which king is credited with having been the author of many of the Old Testament Psalms?**

a. Saul
b. Hezekiah
c. David
d. Jeroboam

10 **He was America's first theologian, the author of *Treatise on Religious Affections* and president of Princeton. What was his name?**

a. Jonathan Edwards
b. Solomon Stoddard
c. George Duffield Jr
d. John Dewey

# AGNOSTICS, SCEPTICS AND ATHEISTS

1 Who claimed that with the 'death' of God man was free to become superman?

2 In which country did Nihilism, the philosophy rejecting established moral, religious and traditional values, have its origin?

3 Of which atheistic philosophical movement was Jean-Paul Sartre a leading light?

4 Who published a collection of his essays in 1957 entitled *Why I am not a Christian*?

5 Which English novelist rejected her early Evangelical upbringing and adopted 'free thinking', translating current critiques of Christianity from German and shocking Victorian society by living with a married man?

6 What nationality was David Hume, the sceptical author of such works as *A Treatise on Human Nature* and *An Enquiry Concerning Human Understanding*?

7 How did Charles Darwin, the leading originator of the theory of evolution by natural selection, describe his own religious beliefs?

8 Who said, 'By night an atheist half believes a God'?

9 Who has recently written, 'It is said in the Bible that the love of money is the root of all evil. It might be truer to say that the love of God is the root of all evil. Religion is the tragedy of mankind'?

10 Who expressed the view that religion 'is the opium of the people'?

# CROSS SECTION

1 **Which flower is attributed to St David?**
  a. Daffodil
  b. Bluebell
  c. Crocus
  d. Primrose

2 **Which prophet found himself transported by the hand or spirit of the Lord?**
  a. Ezekiel
  b. Jeremiah
  c. Moses
  d. Isaiah

3 **Who was walking to Emmaus with a friend on the day of the resurrection when they were joined by a fellow traveller who turned out to be the risen Christ?**
  a. Cornelius
  b. Crispus
  c. Judas
  d. Cleopas

4 **After what event did the Holy Family return from Egypt?**
  a. The Roman census
  b. The visit from the Magi
  c. The death of Herod
  d. The death of Augustus

5 **Who was the author of *Let Our Children Go!*, which opposed the influence of certain religious cults on their young followers?**
  a. Jim Jones
  b. Harvey Cox
  c. Ted Patrick
  d. Gabriel Marcel

6 **In the eighth century a controversy raged in the Eastern Church over the use of images in church. What were the destroyers of images called?**

a. Heretics
b. Iconoclasts
c. Philistines
d. Passionists

7 **Who, 'in all his glory', does Jesus say was no match for 'the lilies of the field'?**

a. Nabob
b. Solomon
c. Nebuchadnezzar
d. David

8 **What is a triquetra?**

a. A weapon
b. A means of transport
c. Part of the Temple furnishings
d. An ornamental symbol of the Trinity

9 **In 1971 Pope Paul VI set an age at which cardinals were obliged to retire from curial offices and from taking part in papal elections. What age was that?**

a. 65
b. 70
c. 75
d. 80

10 **Psalm 17 is the shortest of the psalms. How many verses does it have?**

a. 1
b. 2
c. 3
d. 4

# THE TWELVE TRIBES

1 The opening verse of the Shema, 'Hear, O Israel. The Lord Our God is one Lord' was spoken originally by whom?

2 Which pharaoh do scholars believe was the pharaoh of the Exodus?

3 Who was Israel's first patriarch?

4 Who were they fighting when Saul and Jonathan were killed in a battle on Mount Gilboa, after which David became king?

5 Under whose leadership did the Israelites take possession of Canaan, the Promised Land?

6 Who was Ahab's wife?

7 Under what circumstances was the Ark of the Covenant lost?

8 Who issued a decree allowing the Jews to return to Palestine and rebuild their temples after the Babylonian exile?

9 Who succeeded David as King of Israel?

10 Who was the father of the Jewish hero, Judas Maccabaeus, whose exploits are described in the Books of Maccabees?

# CROSS SECTION

1 **What is the predominant religious faith in Lithuania?**
a. Lutheranism
b. Russian Orthodoxy
c. Roman Catholicism
d. Judaism

2 **What did Jesus say to his disciples as they tried to prevent youngsters in the crowd from getting a closer view when he was teaching in Judea?**
a. 'Harden not your hearts'
b. 'O ye of little faith'
c. 'I have compassion on the multitude'
d. 'Suffer the little children to come unto me'

3 **Which Old Testament book comes between Numbers and Joshua?**
a. Deuteronomy
b. Leviticus
c. Job
d. Ezra

4 **To which world-wide 'church' do Moonies belong?**
a. Holy Spirit Church
b. Children of God
c. Church of Scientology
d. Unification Church

5 **Which Jewish leader, originally a farmer, led a successful campaign against the marauding Midianites?**
a. Joshua
b. Gideon
c. Jonathan
d. Samuel

6 **The pope is sometimes referred to as the Vicar of . . . Can you supply the missing word or words?**
a. Christ
b. Rome
c. St Peter's
d. The Vatican

7 **In the Old Testament there are two men named Uriel. The same name also occurs in the Old Testament Apocrypha. Who or what is called Uriel in that case?**

a. A city
b. A pagan god
c. An angel
d. A mountain

8 **In Mark's Gospel Jesus cures a blind man. What is the first thing the blind man sees?**

a. The sky
b. Jesus's face
c. A dazzling light
d. People that look like trees walking

9 **How often did a sabbatical year recur in Israel?**

a. Every 10 years
b. Every 4 years
c. Every 12 years
d. Every 7 years

10 **When was it revealed that the Turin Shroud showed a very detailed picture of a man who seemed to have died in a manner very similar to that suffered by Jesus?**

a. 1978
b. 1924
c. 1898
d. 1990

# THE CANON AND NOT THE CANON

1 In the Protestant Bible, how many books make up the Old Testament?

2 Traditionally, the Old Testament books are divided into three groups. What are they called?

3 What is the name given by Protestants to additional books found in the Roman Catholic and Eastern Orthodox Bibles?

4 Who in the New Testament refers to the many who 'have undertaken to compile a narrative of the things which have been accompished among us'?

5 When a library was discovered at Nag Hammadi, a 'Gospel' came to light containing many sayings beginning 'Jesus said'. What is the Gospel called?

6 Which Epistle is believed to be the earliest of Paul's letters, dating from around AD 50?

7 Which is thought to be the earliest Gospel?

8 What are the Synoptic Gospels?

9 The Books of Job, Proverbs, Ecclesiastes and, in the Roman Catholic Bible, Wisdom of Solomon and Sirach are all included in a group referred to as what?

10 Why, according to legend, is the earliest translation of the Hebrew Bible into Greek called the Septuagint?

# ANSWERS

**CROSS SECTION Page 10**
1 Rome.
2 Passover.
3 150.
4 William Penn.
5 Zoar.
6 Matthew.
7 Canada.
8 Tübingen.
9 White.
10 Judges.

**THE CHRISTIAN CALENDAR Page 12**
1 Ash Wednesday.
2 4.
3 23 April.
4 Epiphany.
5 6 December (St Nicholas).
6 Christmas.
7 Twelve - Wednesday, Friday and Saturday of each of the four Ember Weeks.
8 25 March - the traditional date of the Annunciation, taken to be New Year's Day.
9 Christmas Day, Good Friday, Easter Day, Ascension Day, Whit Sunday.
10 Fig Sunday.

**CROSS SECTION Page 13**
1 The Jerusalem Bible.
2 Henry VIII.
3 Malcolm Boyd.
4 Syria.
5 My messenger.
6 Henry George Liddell.
7 Judah.
8 Jesus.
9 Betsy Ross.
10 The Amish.

**THIS IS YOUR LIFE Page 15**
1 33 days.
2 Jesse Jackson.
3 William Laud.
4 He resigned his ministry.
5 Il Francesco (The Frenchman) or St Francis as we know him.
6 1950.
7 Ian Paisley.
8 The Oxford Movement.
9 Karol Jozef Wojtyla.
10 St Albans.

**CROSS SECTION Page 16**
1 Via Dolorosa.
2 John T. Scopes.
3 After the Latin for a spring of water.
4 95.
5 Gabon.
6 Maximilian Kolbe.
7 Calcutta (Bishop Daniel Wilson).
8 Bedford.
9 *Church Times*
10 C. S. Lewis.

**MISSIONS OVERSEAS Page 18**
1 St James the Greater.
2 St Francis Xavier.
3 David Livingstone.
4 St Aidan.
5 Bartolome de Las Casas.
6 Gladys Aylward.
7 50 percent.
8 Georgia.
9 St Barnabas.
10 Albert Schweitzer.

**CROSS SECTION Page 19**
1 Charles Andrews.
2 King David.
3 Three days and three nights.
4 Trevor Howard.
5 St Leonard.
6 The unicorn.
7 Samaritans.
8 Diligence.
9 Jethro.
10 Milan.

**SAINTS ALIVE Page 21**
1 St Edward the Confessor.
2 Russia and Greece.
3 The lily, signifying purity.
4 St Anthony of Padua.
5 St Augustine of Canterbury.
6 St Augustine of Hippo.
7 Palestine.
8 St Helena.
9 St Hilda.
10 'Dearest'.

**CROSS SECTION Page 22**

1 Ur.
2 East of Eden.
3 Nunc Dimittis.
4 Benedictine.
5 Myra.
6 Robert Raikes.
7 Nimrod.
8 China.
9 Lepanto.
10 The Holy Grail.

**CHRISTIANITY IN ART Page 24**

1 Salvador Dali.
2 Michelangelo.
3 Tapestry.
4 William Blake.
5 A riza.
6 Henry Moore.
7 Barbara Hepworth.
8 Cappadocia.
9 She is black.
10 William Holman Hunt.

**CROSS SECTION Page 25**

1 5.
2 Athens.
3 James Moffatt.
4 Khruschev.
5 Gopher.
6 The number of the beast.
7 The Society of Friends.
8 St Clare.
9 Charles Wesley.
10 6 January.

**OLD TESTAMENT PROPHETS Page 27**

1 A burning coal from the altar (Isa 6.6).
2 She was persistently unfaithful to him, an analogy of Israel's relationship with God (Hos. 1-3).
3 Four: 'the appearance of the fourth is like a son of the gods' (Dan. 3.25).
4 Micah (5.2).
5 Jeremiah (13.23).
6 The bones are transformed back into living beings 'an exceedingly great host' (Ezek. 37.1-10).
7 God had told him to go to Nineveh and preach against the wickedness of its inhabitants.
8 Lot, Abraham's nephew (Gen. 19.36-7).
9 The whirlwind (Hos. 8.7).
10 Isaiah (2.4).

**CROSS SECTION Page 28**

1 25.
2 Corpus Christi.
3 St John of the Cross.
4 1928.
5 7.
6 Augustus.
7 1970.
8 Moriah.
9 Thou shalt not bear false witness.
10 New York.

**WORDS OF WISDOM Page 30**

1 Dietrich Bonhoeffer.
2 St Thomas Aquinas.
3 Soren Kierkegaard.
4 St Augustine of Hippo.
5 James Cone.
6 Anonymous.
7 Martin Luther.
8 St Julian.
9 Paul Tillich.
10 John Calvin.

**CROSS SECTION Page 31**

1 German.
2 Jericho.
3 Fatima.
4 Frances Xavier Cabrini.
5 191 years.
6 Hadrian VII.
7 Christian Mission.
8 1972.
9 Samuel Mars (the others were all famous Quakers).
10 Cyril and Methodius.

**MIRACLES AND VISIONS Page 33**

1 'Moses stretched out his hand over the sea; and the Lord drove the sea back and the waters were divided' (Exod.14.21).
2 Stigmata.
3 Sleeping (Matt. 9.24, Mark 4.39, Luke 8.52).
4 Seeing and/or experiencing God directly.
5 They were enabled to speak in other tongues to the 'devout men of every nation' so that 'each one heard them speaking in his own language' (Acts 2.5-6).
6 The Virgin bade Bernadette drink from a spring which then miraculously appeared.
7 12 (Matt. 15.34, Mark 8.5-7).
8 White, red, black and 'pale' (Rev. 6.1-8).
9 1 That the wheel on which she was tortured broke through divine intervention.
  2 That her body was transported by angels to Mount Sinai.
10 The angel Gabriel (Luke 1.26-35).

**CROSS SECTION Page 34**

1 Psalms.
2 Abraham's Bosom.
3 St Martin of Tours.
4 *The Cross and The Switchblade.*
5 Index of Prohibited Books.
6 William Brewster.
7 Leah.
8 Dan.
9 John Wycliffe.
10 All Souls' Day.

**WHO SAID? Page 36**

1 St Bede.
2 Thomas à Kempis.
3 1 Corinthians (13.11)
4 Martin Luther.
5 John Milton's.
6 'My God, My God, why hast thou forsaken me?' (Matt 27.46).
7 Mr Collins, in *Pride and Prejudice* by Jane Austen.
8 Thomas Cranmer.
9 Martin Luther King's.
10 St Peter (Acts 3.6).

**CROSS SECTION Page 37**

1 Matthias.
2 *Decision.*
3 7.
4 Henry Purcell.
5 1870.
6 Scientology.
7 Absalom.
8 Huguenots.
9 Codex Sinaiticus.
10 In a chariot of fire.

**THE CHRISTIAN HERITAGE: CHURCHES Page 39**

1 Perpendicular.
2 Parishioners form a ring around a church by holding hands, circling it in a dance or procession on feast days, as part of the celebrations.
3 Greensted, Essex (St Andrew's, built around 845).
4 The rood was an old name for a cross or crucifix which was placed on a beam spanning the nave, below which was a carved screen at the entrance to the chancel.
5 William the Conqueror, who vowed he would do so if victorious over King Harold and the English army.
6 By looking at the mass dial a form of sundial with lines denoting the times of services.
7 The late seventeenth century.
8 The Doom.
9 'Wool churches'.
10 The bicentenary of the birth of the naturalist Gilbert White, a native and in his latter years curate of Selborne.

**CROSS SECTION Page 40**

1 Pietà.
2 After the Latin for a seal.
3 In the sacristy.
4 Manchester, New York.
5 River Nile turning to blood.
6 14.
7 Fisherman.
8 Hagia Sophia.
9 Psalm 100.
10 Gerard Manley Hopkins.

**THE WORLD OF THE BIBLE Page 42**

1 Mount Horeb (Exod. 3.1).
2 It was used to dispose of rubbish and waste, where it was burnt (Matt. 18.9).
3 Mount Nebo, in the land of Moab (Deut. 34.1-5).
4 The Roman Empire.
5 Babylon (2 Kings 24.18-25, 30 and Jer. 52.1-34).
6 On the island of Malta (Acts 28.1).
7 Carmel (1 Kings 18.19-20).
8 The City of David (Luke 2.4).
9 The Dome of the Rock.
10 Jacob's well.

**CROSS SECTION Page 43**

1 Annas.
2 A ship.
3 Jesse.
4 Belshazzar.
5 Eighth.
6 Cana.
7 Linus.
8 Insurrection *and* murder.
9 Jacob Epstein.
10 YMCA.

**CRUSADES Page 45**

1 From the cross worn on their clothing.
2 Turkish.
3 8: the first in 1096, the last ended in 1272.
4 The Albigenses of France.
5 The Children's Crusade.
6 Richard 'The Lionheart'.
7 The Order of the Knights Templar.
8 The Knights Hospitallers of St John of Jerusalem.
9 The massacre and harassment of Jews by Crusaders passing through German towns such as Worms and Mainz.
10 The Turin Shroud.

**CROSS SECTION Page 46**

1 *The Plain Truth.*
2 Knock.
3 Heel.
4 Balsam.
5 As symbols of divine wisdom.
6 Austria.
7 Shiloh.
8 Emanuel Swedenborg.
9 St Peter's, Rome.
10 Zebedee.

**BORN AGAIN Page 48**

1 St Peter's (Acts 2.32-41).
2 Charles Munroe Schultz.
3 Nicodemus (John 3.3).
4 Sixteen.
5 Paul was blind for three days; Ananias helped him regain his sight (Acts 9.9-19).
6 The nineteenth-century American revivalist Charles Furney. The 'anxious bench' was placed at the front of the auditoria during his meetings.
7 Cliff Richard. Dylan returned to his original Jewish faith in the 1980s.
8 Early Pentecostals.
9 'Televangelism'.
10 The Book of Common Prayer. Public Baptism of Such as are of Riper Years.

**CROSS SECTION Page 49**

1 The builders suddenly began speaking in different languages.
2 969.
3 Prague.
4 West.
5 St Sebastian.
6 Blindness.
7 Liverpool.
8 Henry VIII.
9 Ham.
10 Amsterdam.

**MARTYRS REMEMBERED Page 51**

1 A leader of the English Lollard movement following the teachings of Wycliffe. Oldcastle was hanged and burned for his part in the Lollard uprisings.
2 St Stephen (Acts 7.58-60).
3 Thrown to the lions.
4 Poland.
5 John Foxe.
6 Nero.
7 The Boxer rebellion.
8 St Thomas à Becket.
9 The Ugandan martyrs, 22 African Christians who were put to death in the 1880s by King Mwanga for refusing to renounce their faith.
10 Hugh Latimer, Nicholas Ridley and Thomas Cranmer.

**CROSS SECTION Page 52**

1 St Brendan.
2 Nimbus.
3 Herodias.
4 Zadok.
5 7.
6 St Basil's.
7 Romans (6.20-3).
8 By the pool named Bethesda.
9 John Stainer.
10 15 July.

**CHRISTIANITY GOES TO HOLLYWOOD Page 54**

1 Yul Brynner.
2 Audrey Hepburn.
3 Victor Mature.
4 Max von Sydow.
5 Genesis.
6 Eric Liddell.
7 St Matthew.
8 The Virgin Mary.
9 They have all played priests.
10 Satan.

**CROSS SECTION Page 55**

1 Aaron.
2 Santiago de Compostela.
3 Campanile.
4 Norway.
5 Castel Gandolfo.
6 St Chad.
7 St Thomas the Apostle.
8 Jehovah's Witnesses.
9 Cherubim.
10 25 April.

**ALL GOD'S PEOPLE Page 57**

1 Christianity.
2 The Copts of Egypt.
3 The Waldenses (or Waldensians or Vauclois).
4 'Exclusive'or 'Close', and 'Open'.
5 The Benedictine.
6 Moroni.
7 'Elderly woman'.
8 The Shakers.
9 Iona.
10 The Tai Ping rebellion.

**CROSS SECTION Page 58**

1 1740-50.
2 Michelangelo.
3 Shepherd.
4 St Peter.
5 Hadrian IV (Nicolas Breakspear).
6 All of the arms are of the same length.
7 University of California at Los Angeles.
8 Dorothy Day.
9 Fixing votive candles.
10 45 cm.

**CRIES OF THE OPPRESSED Page 60**

1 Constantine.
2 Priest-holes.
3 Rhode Island.
4 Martin Luther King.
5 *A Theology of Liberation* by Gustavo Gutierrez, a Peruvian priest.
6 They all referred to God as Mother giving the Deity a female identity.
7 Marxism.
8 *Uncle Tom's Cabin.*
9 The Disappeared.
10 The Diaspora.

**CROSS SECTION Page 61**

1 Hiram Bingham.
2 Date of Easter.
3 Nicholas Ferrar.
4 Samuel Wilberforce.
5 Wednesday before Good Friday, the day on which Judas Iscariot betrayed Christ.
6 Alleluia.
7 Presentation of Christ in the Temple.
8 St Francis of Assisi.
9 Emperor Constantine.
10 Jamestown.

**DUST TO DUST Page 63**

1 '. . . any that die unbaptized, or excommunicate, or have laid violent hands upon themselves.'
2 Stoke Poges, Buckinghamshire.
3 Joseph of Arimathea (Matt 27.57-60).
4 Robin Hood's lieutenant, Little John.
5 Isolating those suffering from the plague.
6 Highgate cemetery.
7 Four days (John 11.17).
8 Yew.
9 A pyramid.
10 Boot Hill, Dodge City, Kansas.

**CROSS SECTION Page 64**

1 John Milton (in *Paradise Lost*).
2 Edinburgh.
3 Thomas à Becket, the others were three of his assassins.
4 Phoebe.
5 Holding bread at the celebration of the Eucharist.
6 Asia.
7 Emperor Haile Selassie.
8 Scripture Union.
9 Thomas Tallis.
10 Free Church of Scotland.

**ONWARD CHRISTIAN WOMEN Page 66**

1 St Paul (1 Cor. 11.13).
2 Women's Christian Temperance Union, founded in Cleveland, Ohio in 1874.
3 At the General Synod of the Church of England on 11 November 1992.
4 Martha, sister of Mary and Lazarus'.
5 Dorothy L. Sayers. Perhaps the best known of these works is *The Man Born to be King*, first broadcast by the BBC in 1942.
6 Mahalia Jackson.
7 Elizabeth Barton, a domestic servant living at Aldington, who gained celebrity status for her visions and prophecies.
8 Catherine.
9 For the building and restoring churches.
10 Elizabeth Fry, *Observations on the Visiting, Superintending and Government of Female Prisoners.*

**CROSS SECTION Page 67**

1 The sons of Zebedee.
2 Uz.
3 Prague.
4 Sabine Baring-Gould.
5 India.
6 Saul and Jonathan.
7 Mount Athos.
8 They lived on the tops of pillars.
9 Sermon on the Mount.
10 El Salvador.

**SONG OF PRAISE Page 69**

1 Christina Rossetti.
2 1861.
3 Graham Kendrick.
4 'Silent Night'.
5 Mrs Cecil Frances Alexander (1818-95).
6 The Shakers.
7 On the story of Christ's appearances to two disciples on the road to Emmaus. One says to Jesus, 'Abide with us, for it is toward evening and the day is now far spent' (Luke 24.29).
8 'Rock of ages, cleft for me'.
9 Sidney Carter.
10 Sir John Betjeman, 'Hymn'.

**CROSS SECTION Page 70**

1 Los Angeles.
2 Durham.
3 Eight.
4 Matthew and Luke.
5 1928.
6 Evangelical Church.
7 Oxford.
8 29 September.
9 7.
10 Fourth finger of the right hand.

**HOLY WRIT Page 72**

1 From the Greek word *biblia*, meaning 'books'.
2 Hebrew, Aramaic and Greek.
3 Qumran.
4 One of the first Latin Bibles, this version was translated by Jerome in the fourth century into Latin from the original languages.
5 Worms, Germany. Unauthorized versions were forbidden by the Church in England.
6 1611.
7 Because English printers had exclusive copyright on the Authorized, or King James' Version.
8 This Bible was printed in 1810 and the passage in Matthew 13.43 which should have read, 'Who hath ears to hear' in fact read, 'He who hath ears to ear'.
9 Noah Webster.
10 The smallest Bible in the world, published by Oxford University Press in 1896. With some 900 pages, it was only half an inch thick.

**CROSS SECTION Page 73**

1 Sheer Thursday.
2 Alabama.
3 5500.
4 Uganda.
5 St Herman.
6 Bible Sunday.
7 Hampton Court Conference.
8 St Monica.
9 Advent.
10 Great Friday.

**ACTS OF THE APOSTLES Page 75**

1 Theophilus.
2 Probably the author of the third Gospel, St Luke.
3 The stoning of Stephen (Acts 7.58; 8.1).
4 Andrew (Matt. 4.18).
5 Philip (Acts 8. 9-13).
6 The centurion Cornelius, who had fallen at the apostle's feet and worshipped him (Acts 10.25-6).
7 The direct link with Christ and his teachings through the Apostles by the laying on of hands at ordination.
8 Mount Olivet.
9 Phillippi.
10 John.

**CROSS SECTION Page 76**

1 Third Thursday after Easter.
2 Sovereign.
3 1846.
4 John Kennedy.
5 Zaire.
6 Amsterdam.
7 Study of being.
8 Cosmo Gordon Lang.
9 Bath and Wells.
10 Salvation.

**THE CHRISTIAN WORLD TODAY Page 78**

1 Spain.
2 The Board for Social Responsibility.
3 For homosexual and sympathizing Christians.
4 Wycliffe Bible Translators.
5 Mikhail Gorbachev.
6 *The Church and the Bomb.*
7 *Humanae Vitae.*
8 *Faith in the Countryside.*
9 Archbishop Desmond Tutu.
10 David Jenkins.

**CROSS SECTION Page 79**

1 7.
2 Church of God in Christ.
3 A man.
4 Charlemagne.
5 Joseph of Arimathea.
6 Agape.
7 A huge bronze bowl in the precincts of Solomon's Temple.
8 The fourth Sunday in Lent.
9 Shunning.
10 Catholicos.

**FATHER BROWN AND FRIENDS Page 81**

1 *The Innocence of Father Brown* (1911).
2 Upon his own father, Thomas Butler, Rector of Langar, Nottinghamshire.
3 Dr Primrose.
4 The monk's name is Brother William of Baskerville and one of the Sherlock Holmes' stories is *The Hound of the Baskervilles.*
5 Charles Dickens - he is describing Mr Chadband in *Bleak House.*
6 Dr Proudie.
7 Mary Crawford.
8 *Joseph Andrews.*
9 George Eliot.
10 Mexico.

**CROSS SECTION Page 82**

1 2.
2 Adam.
3 Because he touched the Ark.
4 A group of black gospel singers.
5 They abstained from alcoholic drink.
6 Solomon's Seal.
7 7.
8 Latimer's.
9 Joppa.
10 God with us.

**FOUR FOR THE GOSPEL MAKERS Page 84**

1 In chapters 1 to 4 and 26 the Israelite tribes are enumerated.
2 Three.
3 Twelve (Gen. 49.28).
4 Ten: five wise, five foolish (Matt 25. 1-2).
5 Seven (Prov. 9.1).
6 'I say not unto thee, until seven times: but, until seventy times seven.'
7 Two: Baptism and the Eucharist.
8 Seven: Baptism, Eucharist, Confirmation, Penance, Orders, Matrimony and Extreme Unction.
9 The ninth hour.
10 Ten (Exod. 7-11)

**CROSS SECTION Page 85**

1 Stone seats set into the wall for the clergy.
2 The fiftieth day.
3 Sea of Tiberias.
4 Syriac.
5 Exegesis.
6 The letter 'T'.
7 Canterbury.
8 Raven.
9 Unbelief.
10 Nicodemus.

**POWER AND THE GLORY Page 87**

1 Christ Church (originally Cardinal's College).
2 Henry II.
3 Rodrigo Borgia.
4 Democratic Unionist.
5 Cardinal Richelieu.
6 1981.
7 Archbishop Makarios.
8 Jerry Falwell.
9 Rasputin.
10 Bishop Fulton F. Sheen.

**CROSS SECTION Page 88**

1 128.
2 385.
3 Matthew.
4 First Sunday in Lent.
5 Florence.
6 Micah.
7 Swiss.
8 To be fruitful and multiply.
9 Converts from Judaism.
10 It was sacrificed.

**LET US PRAY Page 90**

1 1955.
2 Marcel Lefebvre.
3 From the Greek word meaning 'thanksgiving'.
4 '...the Common Prayers in the Church, commonly called Divine Service' (The Preface to the Book of Common Prayer).
5 The Liturgy of the Word and the Liturgy of the Eucharist.
6 The fourth century.
7 It gathers or collects up the individual prayers and petitions of the congregation into one prayer.
8 A litany of praise said or sung to the Persons of the Holy Trinity, e.g. 'Glory to the Father, and to the Son and to the Holy Spirit'.
9 The 'comfortable words'.
10 The Epistle to the Hebrews.

**CROSS SECTION Page 91**

1 Raphael.
2 Anglican.
3 Philippians.
4 Mark.
5 St Peter's, Rome.
6 Noah and the Flood.
7 Bethany.
8 Molech.
9 Rachmaninoff.
10 Because David's wife Abigail called herself his handmaid.

**THE CHRISTIAN HERITAGE: CATHEDRALS Page 93**

1 Marc Chagall.
2 They were placed in such an open space to resist any inward thrust from the side members.
3 Seville.
4 The 'principia' or headquarters of the Roman settlement.
5 The Great Fire of London (1666).
6 Michelangelo.
7 Antonio Gaudi.
8 Chartres.
9 Sir Basil Spence.
10 Edward the Confessor's Westminster Abbey.

**CROSS SECTION Page 94**

1 Judas.
2 Uruguayan.
3 1650.
4 Gideons.
5 Third Epistle of John.
6 Joses.
7 Revd Barbara Harris.
8 Baroque.
9 Luther.
10 1988.

**OBERAMMERGAU TO THE OLD VIC Page 96**

1 Corpus Christi.
2 Death.
3 The villagers gathered in the parish church whilst the Black Death raged in their midst and vowed to perform a play every ten years in return for God's mercy in their present plight.
4 Sybil Thorndike.
5 Tim Rice.
6 Paul Scofield.
7 It is rescued by angels and borne up to heaven.
8 The Canterbury Festival.
9 *A Boy with a Cart.*
10 *Godspell.*

**CROSS SECTION Page 97**

1 Czestochowa.
2 Ira David Sankey.
3 Swiss.
4 800.
5 Olney.
6 His baptism by John the Baptist.
7 Antioch.
8 St Christopher.
9 Dome of the Rock.
10 Franciscan.

**WHO'S WHO IN THE NEW TESTAMENT Page 99**

1 The two disciples, James and John (Mark 3.17).
2 Caiaphas.
3 This would refer to her home, Magdala, a city to the west of the Sea of Galilee.
4 This early Christian couple sell their property in order, ostensibly, to give the proceeds to the church. They retain some for themselves, however, and seek to deceive Peter about this. As a result they are both struck down and die (Acts 5.1-11).
5 Aquila and Priscilla (Acts 18.1-13, 18; 1 Cor. 16.19; Rom. 16.3).
6 Herod Antipas, the tetrarch, son of Herod the Great (Matt. 14.1-12).
7 Felix (Acts 24.23-7).
8 Zechariah.
9 About 84.
10 Mark.

**CROSS SECTION Page 100**

1 Hannah.
2 Templars.
3 Dogs.
4 Jericho.
5 Andrew.
6 Aaron.
7 First.
8 Cardinal Newman.
9 *Honest to God.*
10 4.

**CHASUBLES, COPES AND KEYS**
**Page 102**

1 The Greek word for a fish, translated, is 'Ichthus'. This was used as an acrostic for Jesus' titles: *Iesus* (Jesus); *Christos* (Christ); *Theou* (of God); *Uios* (Son); *Soter* (Saviour).
2 St Matthew's is an angel, St Mark's is a winged lion, St Luke's is a winged ox, and St John's is an eagle.
3 Jesus assigns 'the keys of the kingdom' to Peter after the disciple has recognized Christ as the Messiah (Matt. 16.19).
4 Red, which symbolized energy and life.
5 When Jesus was baptized the heavens opened and the Holy Spirit descended in the shape of a dove.
6 They have developed from the original Roman style of dress such as the long tunic and stole.
7 The clover.
8 They greeted the dawning of light and symbolized watchfulness.
9 It was associated in myth with virgins, hence the connection with the Virgin Mary.
10 Three.

**CROSS SECTION Page 103**

1 Wild honey.
2 Bathsheba.
3 Leipzig.
4 Moscow.
5 1928.
6 Obadiah.
7 '. . . for they shall be called the children of God.'
8 Midian.
9 Rahab and her family.
10 The Magi.

**MASSES, PASSIONS AND SPIRITUALS**
**Page 105**

1 Miriam (Exod. 15.20-21).
2 *Israel in Egypt* by Georg Friedrich Handel.
3 Monteverdi.
4 St Cecilia is the patron saint of music.
5 Mozart.
6 Black and white spirituals.
7 They were derived from liturgical texts put together by Pope Gregory I in the late sixth century.
8 The famous American gospel singer, trombonist and hymn book publisher.
9 Mendelssohn.
10 A fourteenth-century miracle play.

**CROSS SECTION Page 106**

1 Timisoara.
2 Erasmus.
3 The fall of Smyrna (Izmir) in 1922.
4 7.
5 The Holy Door.
6 New York.
7 Seventh-Day Adventists.
8 Baltimore.
9 The Witch of En-Dor.
10 Jeremiah.

**LIFE OF CHRIST Page 108**

1 8 days old.
2 Eighteen.
3 Because he was short and could not get a good view due to the crowd pressing round Jesus (Luke 19. 1-4).
4 Moses and Elijah (Mark 9.4).
5 The Garden of Gethsemene (Mark 14.32-46).
6 Turning the water into wine at the marriage at Cana (John 2.1- 11).
7 On going into the city they would find a man carrying a jar of water and he would lead them to the room (Mark 14.13-15).
8 The centurion watching Christ as he died (Mark 15.39).
9 He fasts in the wilderness.
10 Simon the Cyrenian (Mark 15.21).

**.CROSS SECTION Page 109**

1 France.
2 Mourning.
3 First Sunday after Easter.
4 He was the First black Anglican Bishop of Nigeria..
5 Confessing Church.
6 Paul VI.
7 Coventry.
8 Good News.
9 A nun.
10 Chile and Argentina .

**CHRISTIAN FESTIVALS Page 111**

1 1 November.
2 2 November.
3 'Fat Tuesday'.
4 6 December.
5 As a commemoration of Jesus' act of humility at the Last Supper (John 13.3-10).
6 In the evening, young men take part in a race to catch a cheese rolling down the very steep side of Cooper's Hill. The custom is known as Cheese Rolling.
7 Yes, Christmas for example.
8 Bread was made from the first corn to be cut in the harvest and consecrated.
9 The old Anglo-Saxon name for dawn and spring was 'Eostre', or similar forms, whose festival was held at around the same time.
10 At the end of the first Thanksgiving dinner in Plymouth colony 1621, an Indian named Quadequina produced popped corn for the settlers to enjoy.

**CROSS SECTION Page 112**

1 St Brigid.
2 It was disestablished.
3 John.
4 1961.
5 Pope Paul VII, who suggested it to Lou Grade.
6 Paul.
7 Of Faith in the Holy Trinity.
8 Luke.
9 Archbishop Ramsey.
10 Disciples of Christ.

**THE ANGELIC HOST Page 114**

1 Jacob (Gen. 31.12).
2 Christians (1 Cor. 6.3).
3 Gabriel (Luke 1.19).
4 Cherubim (1 Kings 6.23-36).
5 Because Michael and his angels fought the dragon, or Satan, when there was war in heaven (Rev. 12.7-9).
6 Nine.
7 A description of the retreat from Mons was written up in the press by Arthur Machen who used the vivid image of St George and angels holding back the German army. It was so vividly portrayed that the imaginary scene became part of the folklore of World War I.
8 Raphael.
9 His pet dog and Raphael.
10 He believes he is experiencing a vision but when he finds himself free of his chains, past the guards and outside the prison gate he realizes the angel has really rescued him (Acts 12.6-11).

**CROSS SECTION Page 115**

1 The Holy Spirit.
2 John XXIII.
3 1698.
4 Zambia.
5 George Whitefield.
6 In the Temple.
7 Mexico.
8 John Henry Newman.
9 Revelation.
10 He demolished the temple to their god Dagon killing himself and all inside.

**CHURCH ORNAMENTS, SACRED OBJECTS AND TREASURES Page 117**

1 Chalice.
2 It is used for buning incense, sometimes called a 'censer'.
3 Anne Boleyn.
4 Hereford Cathedral.
5 St James the Apostle.
6 A lidded vessel used to contain the bread for the Eucharist.
7 Giotto.
8 The Holy Sepulchre (the tomb where Christ's body was laid) and the site of the crucifixion.
9 Crosier.
10 Sainte-Chapelle.

**CROSS SECTION Page 118**

1 Hermit of the Sahara.
2 They were eaten by birds.
3 *Mysticism.*
4 Act of Faith.
5 Napoleon.
6 Act of Supremacy.
7 2.
8 Pope Gregory I.
9 Orange County, California.
10 It turned into a serpent and devoured the serpents created by the magicians from their rods.

**THE DEVIL AND ALL HIS WORKS Page 120**

1 Adversary.
2 1000 years (Rev. 20.2.8).
3 *The Brothers Karamazov.*
4 Because the devil 'had the power of death' which was now destroyed (Heb. 2.14).
5 *The Screwtape Letters.*
6 To the seventy disciples who have returned from the missions on which he sent them (Luke 10.17-19).
7 Only those with permission to do so from the bishops.
8 Denis Wheatley.
9 Beelzebub.
10 Babylon (Rev.18).

**CROSS SECTION Page 121**

1 Africa.
2 2.
3 The Jewish high court.
4 John Knox.
5 Books of Hours.
6 Judas.
7 Because of his opposition to Hitler and the Nazis.
8 Henry VIII.
9 He struck Jesus and told him to hurry to his death.
10 Dore.

**FOOD AND DRINK Page 123**

1 Instead of Jeremiah 8.22 reading, 'Is there no balm in Gilead', it read 'Is there no treacle in Gilead'.
2 Manna (Exod. 16.31).
3 The Pilgrim Fathers' first Thanksgiving dinner.
4 A pottage of lentils (Gen. 25.29-34).
5 The devil suggests that after Jesus' long fast he could turn some stones into bread (Matt. 4.2-4; Luke 4.2-4).
6 Because it contained a heading in Luke's Gospel referring to the 'parable of the vinegar' rather than the more conventional 'parable of the vineyard'.
7 Roast lamb and bitter herbs in a sauce.
8 It was better - 'thou hast kept the good wine until now' (John 2.10).
9 Sacks of corn (Gen. 42.1-3).
10 It was a fig-tree that bore no fruit for him to eat (Matt. 21.18-19; Mark 11.12-14)

**CROSS SECTION Page 124**

1 New Zealand.
2 Pilgrimage.
3 On the Sea of Galilee.
4 Seoul.
5 A servant of the high priest whose right ear was cut off when Jesus was arrested.
6 1859.
7 Philippi.
8 Start of the Cultural Revolution.
9 Canaan.
10 The soldier who thrust the spear

**TURNS OF PHRASE Page 126**

1 Jesus (Matt. 7.6).
2 The goats go on his left side and the sheep on his right (Matt. 25.32-3).
3 Job (19.20).
4 Wisdom (Prov. 4.7).
5 Paul uses it to describe the resurrection of the body in 1.Corinthians 15.52.
6 Moses (Exod. 21.23-4).
7 'Both shall fall into the ditch' (Matt. 15.14).
8 The parable of the marriage of the king's son (Matt. 21.14).
9 William Blake.
10 Charity, or love (1 Pet. 4.8).

**CROSS SECTION Page 127**

1 Manichees.
2 1701.
3 Salem, Massachusetts.
4 The theology of Thomas Aquinas.
5 Himmler.
6 Psalm 23.
7 They disagreed about taking John Mark with them on a second journey.
8 James II.
9 Nicaragua.
10 Bethlehem.

**THE SECOND COMING Page 129**

1 The coming of Christ again to judge the world.
2 The Millennium.
3 The Seventh-Day Adventists.
4 Jesus is telling his disciples what signs to look for (Matt. 24.29).
5 2 Peter (3.10).
6 The Tympanum was the space between the arch and lintel over the door.
7 The antichrist (1 John 2.18; 2 John 7).
8 Paul (2 Thess. 2. 3-8).
9 Jehovah's Witnesses.
10 Armageddon (Rev. 16.16).

**CROSS SECTION Page 130**

1 1523.
2 Electrocuted by a faulty electric fan.
3 Watchmaker.
4 Hong Kong.
5 *Coracle.*
6 Harrison Ford.
7 'Stir up' are the first two words of the collect for that day.
8 Early underground Christian burial places.
9 Francis of Sales.
10 A Boston minister, author of *Magnalia Christi Americana.*

**HEAVEN AND HELL Page 132**

1 Abraham 'afar off, and Lazarus in his bosom' (Luke 16.22-3).
2 Revelation (21.21).
3 St Paul (1 Cor. 15.51-5).
4 Sheol.
5 *Hamlet.*
6 To one of the criminals crucified with him who asked him to 'remember me when thou comest into thy kingdom' (Luke 23. 42-3).
7 Death, judgement, heaven and hell.
8 Purgatory.
9 Dante.
10 The Gospel according to St John (3.16).

**CROSS SECTION Page 133**

1 Bolshevik Russia.
2 33 per cent.
3 The rise of Protestantism.
4 Because of its liturgical language.
5 To save.
6 Papal infallibility.
7 North America.
8 St Andrew.
9 The prophet Lehi.
10 Christadelphians.

## A CHRISTIAN BESTIARY Page 135

1 A brown cross in the lighter coloured coat.
2 The stag had a shining crucifix amidst its antlers.
3 A lion (Jud. 14. 5-6).
4 Two she-bears (2 Kings 2.23-4).
5 A ram (Gen. 22.13).
6 Camel (Matt. 23.24).
7 A goldfinch, believed to feed on thorns.
8 '.. the foxes, the little foxes, that spoil the vines' (Song of Sol. 2.15).
9 In Job 41.1 it seems to be a crocodile, but elsewhere, in Psalm 104.26 for example, a whale.
10 He had a pet swan which was his constant companion.

## CROSS SECTION Page 136

1 Salisbury.
2 Colombia.
3 Peter.
4 She persuaded her husband, the king of Persia, not to massacre the Jews in his realm.
5 3.
6 Voltaire.
7 J. S. Bach.
8 Abel Muzorewa.
9 Martha.
10 Armenia.

## CONVERTS Page 138

1 Chiang Kai-shek.
2 John Wilmot, Earl of Rochester.
3 Malcolm Muggeridge.
4 The Roman centurion, a gentile convert, who shows utter belief in Jesus' ability to cure his sick servant (Luke 7. 2-9).
5 St Augustine of Canterbury.
6 John Eliot.
7 St Boniface.
8 At a Billy Graham campaign at Earl's Court, London, on 16 June 1966.
9 Judaism; she was born Edith Stein at Breslaw, Poland.
10 Kriss Akabusi.

## CROSS SECTION Page 139

1 Simon's.
2 Destruction.
3 Water.
4 All African Conference of Churches.
5 He heard a still small voice.
6 Germany.
7 Jason.
8 The changing of the substance of bread and wine into the body and blood of Christ during the Eucharist.
9 William Walton.
10 Spices to embalm the body.

## MONASTIC ORDERS Page 141

1 The Poor Clares, the order having been founded by St Clare.
2 The Essenes.
3 St Basil the Great.
4 The Cistercians.
5 Trappist.
6 Franciscan.
7 From the Latin word *frater* meaning 'a brother'.
8 Because they wore a *capuche*, a pointed hood or cowl.
9 Dominicans.
10 Brother Cadfael.

## CROSS SECTION Page 142

1 10.
2 Horse - the other animals traditionally appear in Nativity scenes.
3 Locust.
4 Athens.
5 Gospel of Mark.
6 An animal's horn.
7 Jacob's.
8 In the River Jordan.
9 Brazil.
10 St Lawrence.

**THE HEALING MINISTRY Page 144**

1 Luke (Col. 4.14).
2 He spits onto some clay and mixes it into a paste which he puts on to the man's eyes. After washing the clay away the man finds his sight restored (John 9.6-7).
3 David Livingstone.
4 He felt power or 'virtue' leave him (Luke 8.46).
5 They would fall on the floor.
6 Immersion in the baths fed by water from the miraculous spring.
7 The Order of the Missionaries of Charity.
8 The Greek word used by writers and translators of the Bible is *lepra*, which referred to any unpleasant or disfiguring skin disease. Leprosy as we know it was unknown in that area during biblical times and probably arrived there from Europe in the Middle Ages.
9 Mary Baker Eddy.
10 Three: the widow's son (Luke 7.12-17); Lazarus (John 11. 1-44); Jairus' daughter (Luke 8.41-56).

**CROSS SECTION Page 145**

1 Allan Boesak.
2 Oxford.
3 Colossians.
4 Palaeontology.
5 Hebron.
6 Moral Rearmament.
7 Egypt.
8 William Faulkner.
9 Kobe.
10 Those who had accidentally caused the death of another.

**THE POPES Page 147**

1 St Peter the Apostle.
2 The Lateran Treaty.
3 Pope John Paul I.
4 'Pope Joan'.
5 Paul III.
6 Fourteenth century.
7 John XXIII.
8 Men who claimed to be the Pope but not recognized as such.
9 He confronted Attila the Hun and persuaded him to leave the city and its inhabitants unharmed.
10 Because it is situated on the Mons Vaticanus, one of the seven hills of ancient Rome.

**CROSS SECTION Page 148**

1 Paul.
2 Male children under two years old.
3 Ravens.
4 They marked their doorways with the blood of the Passover lamb.
5 Paraguay.
6 Ur.
7 Achan.
8 St Vitus.
9 Hearing the cock crow.
10 430.

**CHRISTIAN LITERATURE Page 150**

1 The Song of Solomon.
2 Francis Kilvert.
3 John Donne.
4 Emily Dickinson.
5 The medieval poet William Langland.
6 Willa Cather.
7 John Milton's *Samson Agonistes.*
8 *The Robe.*
9 St John of the Cross.
10 Jonathan Swift.

**CROSS SECTION Page 151**

1 A small whip.
2 A means of healing.
3 Galilee.
4 Counter-Reformation.
5 In the second century.
6 Timothy.
7 Warsaw.
8 St Theresa of Lisieux.
9 David.
10 Jonathan Edwards.

**AGNOSTICS, SCEPTICS AND ATHEISTS Page 153**

1 Friedrich Nietzsche.
2 Pre-revolutionary Russia.
3 Existentialism.
4 Bertrand Russell.
5 George Eliot (Mary Ann Evans).
6 He was a Scot (born in Edinburgh in 1711).
7 His views on religion shifted uncertainly but in later life he described himself as 'agnostic'.
8 Edward Young (1683-1765), from his poem *Night Thoughts*.
9 A. N. Wilson, *Against Religion* (1991).
10 Karl Marx.

**CROSS SECTION Page 154**

1 Daffodil.
2 Ezekiel.
3 Cleopas.
4 The death of Herod.
5 Ted Patrick.
6 Iconoclasts.
7 Solomon.
8 An ornamental symbol of the Trinity.
9 80.
10 2.

**THE TWELVE TRIBES Page 156**

1 Moses (Deut. 6.4).
2 Rameses II (circa 1290-1224 BC).
3 Abraham.
4 The Philistines (1 Sam. 31.1-7).
5 Joshua's (The Book of Joshua).
6 Jezebel (1 Kings 16.31).
7 In the destruction of the Temple in Jerusalem when the forces of Nebuchadnezzar sacked the city in 587 BC (2 Kings 25.13-17).
8 Cyrus the Great, King of Persia (Ezra 1.1-2).
9 Solomon (1 Kings 2.10-12).
10 The son of the priest Mattathias, who began a successful revolt against the Syrian ruler, Antiochus IV.

**CROSS SECTION Page 157**

1 Roman Catholicism.
2 'Suffer the little children to come unto me.'
3 Deuteronomy.
4 Unification Church.
5 Gideon.
6 Christ.
7 An angel.
8 People that look like trees walking.
9 Every 7 years.
10 1898.

**THE CANON AND NOT THE CANON Page 159**

1 39.
2 The Law, the Prophets and the Writings.
3 Apocrypha.
4 Luke (Luke 1.1).
5 The Gospel of Thomas.
6 1 Thessalonians.
7 Mark, cAD 70.
8 Matthew, Mark and Luke, John's Gospel seems different to the other three in content and structure.
9 The Wisdom Books.
10 Ptolemy II requested the Jewish leaders to provide 72 scholars to embark on the work of translation; 'Septuagint' refers to this as it is derived from the Latin for 'seventy'.